The Minor Dramatists of Seventeenth-Century Spain

Twayne's World Authors Series

Gerald Wade, Editor

Vanderbilt University

TWAS 653

SEGVNDA PARTE DE

COMEDIAS

ESCOGICASDASDELAS

MEJORES DE ESPAñA.

DEDICADAS

L SEñOR DOCTOR DON FRANCISCO
Ramos del Mançano, del Confejo de fu Mageftad,
en el Real de Caftilla, &c.

CON PRIVILEGIO.

EN MADRID. En la Imprenta Real, Año 1652.

Acofta de Antonio del Ribero, Mercader de Libros.

The Minor Dramatists of Seventeenth-Century Spain

By Vern G. Williamsen

The University of Missouri–Columbia

Twayne Publishers • *Boston*

The Minor Dramatists of Seventeenth-Century Spain

Vern G. Williamsen

Copyright © 1982 by G. K. Hall & Company
Published by Twayne Publishers
A Division of G. K. Hall & Company
70 Lincoln Street
Boston, Massachusetts 02111

Book Production by Marne B. Sultz

Book Design by Barbara Anderson

**Library of Congress Cataloging in
Publication Data**

Williamsen, Vern G.
The minor dramatists of
seventeenth-century Spain.

(Twayne's world authors series ; TWAS
653)
Bibliography: p. 152
Includes index.
1. Spanish drama—Classical period,
1500–1700—History and criticism.
I. Title. II. Series.
PQ6105.W47   862'.3'09   81-7202
ISBN 0-8057-6496-8   AACR2

Contents

About the Author

Vern G. Williamsen received the A.B. degree from San Jose State University in 1948 and, after a successful career as a public school teacher, returned to continue his studies at the University of Arizona, where he received the M.A. degree in 1964. The Ph.D. degree was granted by the University of Missouri in 1968. Professor Williamsen taught at Westminster College in Fulton, Missouri, prior to his appointment to the staff of the University of Missouri at Columbia in 1968, where he is now professor of Spanish.

Besides being a member of several learned societies, Professor Williamsen has served as bibliographer to and as a member of the editorial board for the *Bulletin of the Comediantes*. He has been chairman of the division of the Modern Language Association of America dealing with the early Spanish theater and also of the Spanish I division of the Midwest Modern Language Association. His published research includes several editions of Golden Age plays: Antonio Mira de Amescua's *No hay dicha ni desdicha hasta la muerte* (Columbia, Mo., 1971), the same author's *La casa del tahur* (Chapel Hill, N.C., 1973), and Juan Ruiz de Alarcón's *Don Domingo de Don Blas* (Chapel Hill, N.C., 1975). He has also served as editor for the *Studies in Honor of Ruth Lee Kennedy* (Chapel Hill, N.C., 1977), and as annotator and general editor of the *Annotated, Analytical Bibliography of Tirso de Molina Studies* (Columbia, Mo., 1979). In addition, Professor Williamsen has published extensively in the *Modern Language Journal, Romanische Forschungen, Hispania, Bulletin of the Comediantes, Estudios, Cuadernos Americanos,* and *Hispanófila,* as well as in the *Actas* of the several international conferences he has attended and in several volumes of *comedia* studies. He is actively continuing his research in the field of his greatest interest, the Spanish *comedia* of the Golden Age.

Preface

Any attempt to deal critically with the minor dramatists of Spain's Golden Age explores relatively uncharted waters as a study of the sparse bibliography will prove. In spite of the fact that the extant texts of plays written by nonmajor figures outnumber those of the recognized, important writers of the period, very little work has been done to find out what their works have to offer the literary researcher. The seventeenth-century Spanish dramatists for whom volumes are in print or planned for the Twayne World Authors Series left the astonishing total of nearly 1,400 *comedias*. This forms the field cultivated by most critics working in the area. The approximately 1,750 extant texts left by nearly 100 minor authors (that is, lesser in terms of individual productivity) are rarely read and even more infrequently investigated. Yet there is good reason to doubt that the productivity of the major figures is, in itself, an indication of quality. Although the majority of the major figures are represented by repertoires of between fifty and 100 plays each, two anomalous writers, Juan Ruiz de Alarcón with only twenty-four extant texts, and Lope de Vega, to whom nearly 500 surviving plays are attributed, are a case in point. Both are generally recognized as major playwrights in spite of the fact that while the greater part of Alarcón's relatively small output consists of artistically fine works, the same status cannot be claimed for more than a meager 10 per cent of Lope's *comedia* production. One must, then, ask if there is any reason, other than the sheer mass of the materials available, to ignore such minor dramatists as Andrés de Claramonte, Felipe Godínez, Francisco Bances Candamo, Manuel Vidal Salvador, and Alejandro Arboleda, with more than twenty *comedias* each; Luis Belmonte Bermúdez, Antonio Enríquez Gómez (Fernando de Zárate), Pedro Lanini y Sagredo, and Cristóbal de Monroy y Silva, with more than thirty; or Juan Matos Fragoso and Juan Bautista Diamante, with more than forty extant texts apiece.

Obviously, no short volume such as this is designed to be can attempt to cover so extensive an area with any pretense to thoroughness. It is my intention, instead, to study a representative sampling of the works and workers in order to show that in the very process of creation, the *comedia* became a fixed artistic format with its own set of functional conventions, appurtenant devices, and *ornati*. As the form became more and more a repetitive pattern and the language increasingly came to be a series of poetic clichés, the number of poets and poetasters who attempted to enter the lucrative marketplace with their wares multiplied to a self-destructive extent. Unavoidably, then, as a study of the artistic inventions and beauties found among the works of the numerous writers whose works remain to us, this book must be, even though only in part, a study of the death of an art in the stagnant backwaters of proliferation. This death was brought about as much by the crystallization of the basic structures as by the dystrophy of its decorative covering, the rhetorical language that had at one time turned the underlying skeletons into living, moving creations.

Limitations are imposed on the contents of this book by the space available as well as by the underlying uncertainties of the unknown. No one, to my knowledge, has yet studied all of the texts available. Nor have I. Additionally, this work is confined to those dramatists who wrote *comedias*. Any attempt to extend the study to writers of *autos sacramentales, entremeses,* or other forms of the so-called *teatro menor* (short theater pieces) of that time, would so expand the material as to surpass the limits agreed upon. The same must be claimed as the reason for avoiding the very interesting materials dealing with the origins of the *comedia* as an art form or as a social phenomenon. The limitations are not, therefore, the result of an overpowering sense of the importance of the period that saw the dramatic rose we call the *comedia* come into full bloom, wither with age, and fall into decay, but rather they are imposed partly by my own lack of intellectual daring and by the quite limited space available. It is my hope that the curious reader will make full use of the bibliography included here, in which I have attempted to indicate those articles and books that do treat such fascinating questions more fully. Materials are identified there, as well, indicating sources for further study of the minor dramatists on the part of those wishing to delve into them more deeply.

The basic aim of the book is to introduce the reader to the vast and interesting periphery of the Golden Age *comedia,* a field in which the roots are as yet to be uncovered and whose finest fruits have still not been completely consumed (though they have been tasted). The first chapter will necessarily deal with a definition of the forms and elements that are to be studied. Later chapters will attempt a chronological study of representative processes and successes of the genre and the period, as well as of the artists who prepared them.

As we analyze the structures of the *comedias,* it would be well to bear in mind that any study of this nature may perhaps be compared with that of an artist studying anatomy. He looks first at the skeleton—a rather incongruous object. To do so he strips away the flesh that gives the bones meaning. There remains only the grotesque understructure. Just so, in looking at the dramatic structures underlying the *comedias* approached here, what remains after the artistic material is removed may often seem a strange, unrelated, and comically absurd object. Yet this is only the first step towards the serious critical study that must follow.

Undoubtedly the book will not remain free of faults, unwise omissions, and outright errors for which I ask the reader's indulgence and that he attribute them to my own limitations as I deal with this extensive, yet relatively unexplored area of literary expression.

I wish here to recognize the fact that a sabbatical leave from my duties at the University of Missouri, in the academic year 1974–1975, that was spent in locating and reading primary materials in the Biblioteca Nacional in Madrid, saw the beginning of the work presented here. A Summer Research Grant, a travel grant, and several smaller grants for typing and reproduction expenses, all of which were very generously provided by the Research Council of the Graduate School at the University of Missouri, have provided the funds necessary for the completion of the work.

I also owe a special debt of gratitude to Professor A. David Kossoff, who read my first attempts to solve the problems posed by the materials of this book and made many valuable suggestions, as well as to my friend and colleague Professor Howard Mancing, who read the completed typescript and offered welcome advice. Additionally, all those who have come to hear me read papers on one of the "minor" dramatists at any of the several meetings where they were presented and did, there, offer useful critical commentary, deserve recognition for their part in bringing the work to its present state.

Vern G. Williamsen

The University of Missouri–Columbia

Chronology

1562	Lope de Vega is born in Madrid.
1569	Guillén de Castro is born in Valencia.
1574	Antonio Mira de Amescua is born in Guadix.
1579	Luis Vélez de Guevara is born in Ecija.
1580 or 1581	Gabriel Téllez (Tirso de Molina) born in Madrid.
1581	Juan Ruiz de Alarcón is born in Mexico.
1585–1588	The earliest dated plays of Lope de Vega appear.
1600	Juan Pérez de Montalván is born in Madrid.
1601	Juan Pérez de Montalván is born in Madrid.
1601–1620	Minor dramatists: Miguel Sánchez (died before 1630), Damián Salucio del Poyo (died in 1614), and Andrés de Claramonte (died in 1626).
1604	Performance of Mira de Amescua's *La rueda de la Fortuna* [The Wheel of Fortune] in Toledo.
1605	Publication of *Don Quijote,* Part I.
1607	Francisco de Rojas Zorilla born in Toledo.
1609	Lope de Vega writes his *Arte nuevo de hacer comedias* [The New Art of Writing Plays], and the *comedias: El Acero de Madrid* [The Steel of Madrid] and *Peribáñez.*
1610–1616	The Count of Lemos is in Naples, as viceroy, with his literary court.
1615	Publication of *Don Quijote,* Part II. Tirso de Molina writes his *comedia: Don Gil de las calzas verdes* [Sir Gil of the Green Breeches].
1616	Death of Miguel de Cervantes. Mira de Amescua writes his *comedia: La casa del tahur* [The Gambler's Home].
1618	Augustín Moreto is born in Madrid.

1621   Death of Philip III and the ascension to the throne of his son Philip IV, whose favorite, the Count-Duke of Olivares, will wield the real power.

1621–1630   Minor dramatists: Felipe Godínez (1585–1637), Diego Jiménez de Enciso (1585–1634), and Luis de Belmonte Bermúdez (1587–before 1650).

1623   The earliest plays of Pedro Calderón de la Barca are performed.

1626   Alarcón joins the Consejo de Indias ("Council of the Indies") after writing what is probably the last of his *comedias: Don Domingo de Don Blas.*

1628   Mira de Amescua writes his *comedia: No hay dicha ni desdicha hasta la muerte* [There Is Neither Fortune nor Misfortune until Death].

1631   Calderón writes his *La vida es sueño* [Life Is a Dream]. Lope de Vega writes *El castigo sin venganza* [Punishment without Vengeance]. Guillén de Castro dies.

1631–1650   Minor dramatists: Antonio Hurtado de Mendoza (1586–1644) and Alvaro Cubillo de Aragón (1596–1661).

1632   Mira de Amescua retires to Guadix.

1634   Opening of the court theater El Coliseo del Buen Retiro. Lope writes his *Bizarrías de Belisa* [Belisa's Generosity].

1635   Death of Lope de Vega.

1638   Death of Juan Pérez de Montalván.

1643   The Count-Duke of Olivares falls from favor.

1644   Death of Antonio Mira de Amescua and Luis Vélez de Guevara.

1644–1649   The theaters are closed periodically in mourning for the death of Queen Isabel of Bourbon in 1644 and of Prince Baltasar Carlos in 1646.

1648   Death of Rojas Zorrilla in Madrid and Tirso de Molina in Almazán.

1651   The Coliseo reopens.

1651–1700   Minor dramatists: Agustín de Salazar y Torres (1642–1675), Sor Juana Inés de la Cruz (1651–1695), and Francisco Antonio de Bances y López-Candamo (1662–1704).

1652–1701   The publication of the great collection of Spanish *comedias* known by various titles but collectively as the *Escogidas*.

1667   Death of Philip IV and ascension to the throne of his son Carlos II.

1669   Death of Agustín Moreto.

1681   Death of Pedro Calderón de la Barca.

1700   Death of King Carlos II and the Spanish throne passed to the House of Bourbon.

Chapter One
The *Comedia:* A Question of Genre

The *comedia* must be defined as that full-length drama that was born in Spain during the sixteenth century. It took on various forms, all grown on Spanish soils, fertilized by rather large doses of the Italian Renaissance tradition and the *Commedia dell'Arte,* pollenized by the almost hedonistic atmosphere of the period (an attitude kindled in part by the overrapid influx of New World gold), and brought to fruition under that burning sun of religious fire, the Spanish Counter-Reformation. These, acting in concert, gave such an individual flavor to the Spanish theater as to make it readily distinguishable from that of the rest of Europe. This golden fruit was first picked by Lope de Vega Carpio, who brought it, as he himself admits, to the marketplace. Lope is often referred to as the father of the Spanish National Theater, not because of the more than 1,500 literary children he is said to have given to the stage, but rather because he, practically singlehandedly, brought together the materials from which the *comedia* was made. Like Virués, he wrote his plays in a three-act format; like Gil Vicente, he employed a wide variety of verse forms in polymetric style; and, like Juan de la Cueva, he built his plots around a mixture of tragic and comic elements. The *comedia,* more or less as Lope formed it, held sway from the time he began writing for the stage (around 1585) until the death of the Mexican nun Sor Juana Inés de la Cruz, some hundred years later.

A fine statement about the course of events during that Golden Age of the Spanish drama was written more than a hundred years ago by the German critic Gustav Freytag. He said:

No poetic of a Castilian informs us that the Spanish cloak-and-dagger drama artistically wove the threads of its intrigue . . . according to fixed rules, but we are able to recognize very well many of these rules in the

1

uniform construction of the plays and in the ever-recurring characters; and it would not be very difficult to formulate a code of peculiar rules from the plays themselves. These rules, of course, even to contemporaries, to whom they were useful, were not invariable; through the genius and shrewd invention of individuals, these they gradually learned how to improve and remodel, until the rules became lifeless; and after a period of spiritless application, together with the creative power of the poets, they were lost. [1]

What Freytag did not say was that the structural rules he was writing about were not developed before or concurrently with the *comedia,* but like the rules for musical composition, they grew from the artistic intuition of the masters who employed them. Just as the science of grammar grows from analytical study of how a living language operates, so do these rules by means of which we attempt to explain how an artist creates his work result from an analysis of already completed and successful pieces. These structural rules do serve the very useful purpose of allowing us to see how the artist has achieved that unity within the work which is so necessary to any artistic expression. Yet, once the rules are completely understood by those who follow the master artist in his creation, they inevitably give access to those who would use them as a means toward creation, rather than an understanding of it, even though they lack the necessary genius through which to achieve success. Their efforts are, then, doomed to individual failure, and the overemphasis on such procedures leads to an all too easily recognized effect, the death of the genre that has been thus ossified.

Basic Dramatic Structures

About the only element universally accepted as being basic to the structure of all dramatic art is that of *conflict.* If there is no conflict, there is, by definition, no drama. The minute we attempt to go beyond that point to define dramatic structures, we seem to be entering a land where no two critics speak exactly the same language. Although much has been written about dramatic structure, there is no general agreement even as to the meanings of many of the words employed. Each critic, therefore, must define or redefine the terms he chooses to use. Consequently, even though much of the terminology that will be used in this book may have been utilized elsewhere with different connotations, unless there is a recognized preference for one meaning above another, each should be understood to be used here only within the context in which it is presented.

Freytag, in his monumental study *Techniques of the Drama,* first published in 1863 and then translated from the original German and printed several times during the nineteenth and twentieth centuries (most recently in 1968), proposed that underlying *all* drama was a basic pyramidal structure. He demonstrated his point by analyzing examples from the Classic, Elizabethan, French Neoclassic, and German Romantic theaters. Freytag insisted that the conflict in any play concerns two elements which afflict the protagonist: Those which impinge upon his emotions as they are excited from an internal point or by his own deeds, and those whose source is purely external. He says, in part:

> The structure of the drama must show these two contrasted elements of the dramatic joined in a unity, efflux and influx of will-power, the accomplishment of a deed and its reaction on the soul, movement and counter-movement, strife and counter-strife, rising and sinking, binding and loosing. . . . These two chief parts of the drama are firmly united by a point of the action which lies directly in the middle. This middle, the climax of the play, is the most important place of the structure; the action rises to this; the action falls away from this. It is now decisive for the character of the drama which of the two refractions of the dramatic light shall have a place in the first part of the play, which shall fall in the second part as the dominating influence . . . these two ways of constructing a drama have become characteristic of individual poets and of the time in which they lived.[2]

Freytag goes on from this point to outline the structure of any drama as including the following: introduction, initiating incident or force, rising action, climax, tragic force or incident, falling action, and catastrophe. These may be diagrammed as in Figure 1.

More recently, critics have seemed to accept a variant of Freytag's statement of the pyramidal form or structure of the drama. Apparently they have been influenced by a phenomenon he does not explain adequately, the increasing emotional tension perceived by the audience as the drama proceeds toward its end, toward a climactic point much nearer the end of the play than near the middle. One such critic typical of the rest, Frank H. O'Hara, explains the dramatic structure in terms

DRAMATIC STRUCTURE—FREYTAG

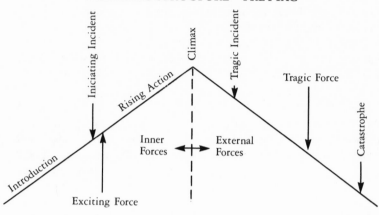

Figure   1

of exposition, inciting moment, development, climax, resolution and denouement.[3] The climax is defined as the moment when the development has taken the play to a point where the resolution of its problem becomes a necessity. The same critics says further:

> When the play has reached its highest height it does exactly what any of us would do after reaching a summit, it starts down again and it comes down faster than it went up. . . . If one thinks of a play as susceptible to diagram, as represented by a scalene triangle, then the apex is certainly the climax. In this geometrical and architectural sense, analyzers have found a definite high point in the construction of every play, a point toward which the rising action is focused and at which the falling action begins. They have frequently described this point as the moment when all the knots are tied and it is impossible to move further without untying a knot.[4]

For the sake of comparison with the diagram of Freytag's conception of dramatic structure, see Figure 2.

In applying the principles elucidated by these two views of dramatic structure, I see that both contain ideas useful to approaching the

DRAMATIC STRUCTURE—O'HARA

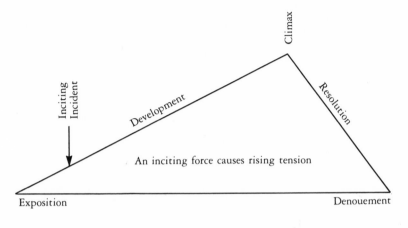

Figure   2

comedia. I prefer, however, to start with the word *plot,* a term that infers *conflict* since that is the raw material from which plot is constructed. Inherent to conflict is the interplay of two opposing forces. At least one of the opposing forces is usually a person. This protagonist may be involved in conflict with the forces of nature, another person, or society itself; or two elements within him may struggle for mastery. "Without *conflict,* without opposition, plot *per se* does not exist."[5] In dealing with plot, it seems preferable to talk in terms of the trajectories traveled by the protagonists rather than to speak of a geometric form such as the pyramid or the triangle. These seem to be too solid, too static for explaining such a dynamic medium as the theater. I view the structure of the *comedia* as consisting of the following elements: exposition *(ex),* initiating incident *(in),* rising action *(ra),* pivotal point *(pp),* tensing action *(ta),* emotional climax *(ec),* resolution *(re),* and denouement *(dt).* The tensing action is characterized by the tension created by opposing a real trajectory *(rt)* and a potential trajectory *(pt)* along which the protagonist moves or seems to move toward opposite ends— to real comedy or apparent tragedy (perhaps the reverse). The divergence between these two possible endings of the play brings about the emotional climax, that point at which the tension resulting from the two possible outcomes cannot be increased further without destroying the work.[6]

In this view of the *comedia*, it is necessary to keep in mind Freytag's description of the forces that act upon the protagonist's trajectory. He suggested that if the motion of the first half of the play were excited by internal forces, the second half would be influenced by forces external to the principal character, and to the contrary. This concept is often useful in understanding the structure of a *comedia*, but does not always explain adequately what happens. Sometimes the forces that shape the path traveled by the protagonist might be better explained as resulting from the conflict of tragic and comic forces, using the words tragic and comic in the sense of Lope de Vega's "The sad and the happy mixed."[7] This use of the terms is in contrast with Lope's usage elsewhere in the same *New Art of Writing Comedias,* where, following the Aristotelian lead, he defines tragedy *(tragedia)* as dealing with historical materials and comedy *(comedia)* as invented material (lines 111–12).

Superimposing the two earlier diagrams in the fashion indicated here, the diagram which results is as in Figure 3.

COMEDIA STRUCTURE

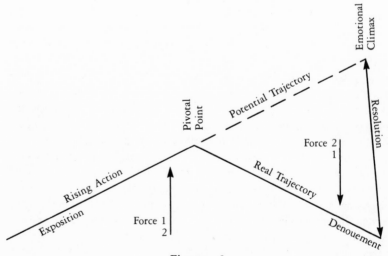

Figure   3

All the other elements that make up any *comedia* relate to this structure. In fact, they relate to the three key points defining the shape of the total trajectory: the initiating incident, the pivotal point, the emotional climax, and through them to the structure as a whole. This in itself is clear proof that the dramatists of the period, either consciously or intuitively, were aware of the strength of such a structure and of its implications for artistic unity. That such an awareness was not completely intuitive we can be sure. Lope, in his *New Art of Writing Comedias,* pointed out the fact that a play is subject to division into three acts, corresponding to the three cardinal points noted above, as well as into symmetrically developed halves.

> Having chosen a subject, write it out in prose
> and divide it into three portions of time.
> ·
> Having divided the plot into two parts,
> connect them from the beginning
> until the movement of the action declines;
> but do not permit the solution
> to be realized until the final scene. (lines 211–
> 35)

When Lope writes of dividing the story into two parts, he is, of course, speaking of the relationship between plot and subplot; however, he does recognize the dual nature of the basic structure when he speaks of the change in the direction of the dramatic movement. He recognized, also, the need for maintaining unity and, at the same time, building suspense, a suspense he himself often supported by means of creating a very real tension between what was truly occurring and what was apparently going to happen. To see how this process operated, let us first take a look at a well-known *comedia* from among the best of the production of the father of the Spanish National Theater, Lope himself, before we pass on to an examination of the works of the minor dramatists.

Peribáñez y el Comendador de Ocaña.   The standard critical view of this play sees the Comendador's forgiveness of Peribáñez after being mortally wounded by him as the emotional climax of the work and the entire following set of scenes in the presence of the King and Queen as being anticlimactic.[8] This, however, seems to me the result either of a modern reading of the seventeenth-century work or a misreading of the underlying structure. The play, written by Lope at about the same time he was preparing the *New Art of Writing Comedias*, demonstrates the validity of the *schema* proposed here. The first half of the *comedia* contains the expository material, the initiating incident, and rising action called for in the model.

As the play begins, Casilda and Peribáñez are celebrating their marriage *(ex)*, when the Comendador, coming to take part in the festivities, falls from his horse in the street outside their door *(in)*. When he is brought into their house for care, he awakens, sees Casilda, and conceives a passionate desire for her *(ra)*, which she coolly but understandingly turns aside. After a beautiful and interesting love scene between the newly married couple *(ex)*, Peribáñez and Casilda plan a trip to celebrate the feast of the Assumption in Toledo *(ra)*. The Comendador, meanwhile, plots to induce Casilda to give in to his desires *(ra)*. While Peribáñez and Casilda are in Toledo, they are permitted to see the King *(ex)*. Although neither is aware of it, the Comendador has a portrait of Casilda prepared from a sketch *(ra)*.

As expected, the second act centers about the pivotal point. Following this key moment, Lope carefully maintains suspense by gradually increasing the tension between the tragic path down which the protagonist seems to be traveling (potential trajectory) and the happy conclusion (real trajectory). This opposition leads to the emotional climax, resolution, and denouement.

Peribáñez returns from Toledo to find that he has been elected to head the *cabildo* (Confraternity of St. Roche) and must take the saint's statue to Toledo for repairs *(ra)*. The Comendador sets up a two-pronged plot to achieve his purpose. He gets Luján to take harvest work with Peribáñez's crew as a means of gaining his own entry to the house. At the same time, he has another underling pretend to propose marriage to Inés, Casilda's cousin, hoping to make use of that relationship to the same end *(ra)*. When he attempts to carry out the first of these plans, Casilda stops him short, refusing even to recognize the Comendador *(pp)*. From this point on (the physical as well as the literary center point of the play), one can be certain that the Comendador will not succeed in gaining Casilda by persuasion. One also feels that if he continues in his attempts, tragedy will result. Lope creates tension through the technique of alternating scenes pointing to this potential tragedy with those that lead inevitably to the real conclusion. Peribáñez sees the portrait of Casilda in Toledo and his jealousy is inflamed *(pt)*. He returns, only to find that Casilda is blameless *(rt)*. The Comendador plots to send Peribáñez off to battle and out of the house *(pt)*. Peribáñez rids himself of the Comendador's previous gifts and insists that the Comendador himself honor him as he takes over the captaincy of the peasant army *(rt)*. The troops leave for war *(pt)*, but Peribáñez has provided himself with a fine horse that he uses to return, unexpectedly, to his house that night *(rt)*. He finds the Comendador inside with Casilda and kills both the nobleman and the traitors who made the entry possible *(pt)*. Peribáñez and Casilda flee *(rt)*. The King, at his court, sets a high price on the head of the Comendador's murderer *(pt)*. Peribáñez and Casilda appear at court to face the inevitable royal justice *(ec)*. Peribáñez asks the King to grant the reward to his wife and offers himself to the King's mercy *(re)*. The King and Queen deal out true justice, honoring Peribáñez and Casilda for the exemplary behavior they have exhibited *(dt)*.

The movement of the plot up to the pivotal point seems to be under the influence of inner forces driving the three main characters. Peribáñez, Casilda, and the Comendador are all forced to act as they do by those drives innate to their natures: Peribáñez by his honor and love for his wife; Casilda by her love for Peribáñez and by her womanly nature (as distasteful as this characterization may seem to a modern reader under the influence of the women's equality movements); and the Comendador by his animal passions. The second half of the play is governed—as Freytag proposed—by contrasting external forces: the painter who prepared Casilda's portrait, the farm laborers who sing a popular *copla* about Casilda's refusal of the Comendador, the King's call at an opportune moment for an army to be raised, and events at the court itself. Equally noteworthy is the way in which Lope accounts for the presence of the King throughout the play, since only the King may grant real honor or deal out ultimate justice. Since his presence in the play is quite open, and since the audience of the time would be quite aware of his position as the source of honor and justice, the real emotional climax of the play for its seventeenth-century audience was not reached with the death of the Comendador but rather when

Peribáñez himself confronts the King. The action in which the pair flee and the dying Comendador refuses to seek vengeance upon them certainly must have been recognized as an emotionally appealing moment, but the real climax for a Lopean audience would have been later. The tension between what could and what would happen increases until the King's presence, well established in the course of the play, is accounted for (see Figure 4).

Other Dramatic Structures

Not all of the plays called *comedias (tragedias* or *tragicomedias)* in seventeenth-century Spain follow the structural pattern just described. Some are, by nature, episodic or linear. Because these generally lack

PERIBAÑEZ Y EL COMENDADOR DE OCAÑA

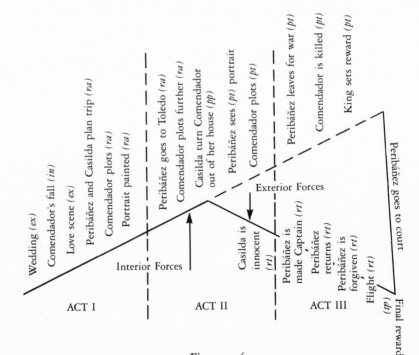

Figure 4

conflict, the prime component of true drama as earlier defined, they are not properly spoken of as drama and should be judged in the light of their own structural principles as subgenres of the *comedia*. [9] The lack of recognition of this fact has led to pejorative criticism of many of these works colored by the realization that they do not measure up to the standard of drama. Other critics have intuitively realized that the piece they are discussing is, indeed, a work of beautiful, masterly conception or presentation, yet they have often found it difficult to justify their intuitive reaction so in contrast with critical tradition. Consequently, repeated attempts have been made to identify the "dramatic unity" and artistic worth of the play in its nondramatic elements: figurative or poetic language, thematic development, or didactic purpose. I contend that a critical process that takes first cognizance of the structure of the work will enable us to comprehend more readily and appreciate better its true value.

Most of the plays that lack the true dramatic infrastructure described above deal with historical, religious, legendary, or mythological themes in such a way that the structure of the piece as well as its theme reflect the ceremonial or ritual purpose of the work. Pomp and circumstance rather than dramatic tension flesh out the underlying linear skeletons of the plays. To illustrate the point I would like to cite here very briefly three plays by Lope de Vega: *Carlos V en Francia* [Charles V in France], *La tragedia del Rey don Sebastián y el bautismo del Príncipe de Marruecos* [The Tragedy of King Sebastian and the Baptism of the Prince of Morocco], and *Las paces de los reyes y judía de Toledo* [The Royal Reconciliation and Jewess of Toledo]. The demonstration of just how critics have sought dramatic value in these three plays through explications of their nondramatic elements will lead us inevitably into the final section of this introductory chapter, a brief exposition of the relationship of other elements to the underlying structures of the *comedia*.

Charles V in France. Act I of the play deals with the meeting of Charles V and Francis I near Nice in 1538, a meeting held under the auspices of Pope Paul III. Act II takes place in Toledo later that same year. Lope chooses to center the act around the justice imposed by Charles in the case of the Duke of the Infantado, who had wounded a bailiff *(alguacil),* rather than deal substantially with the more important but dramatically less interesting meeting of the Cortes (1538–39).

The third act portrays Charles's short stay in Paris, January 1 to 7, 1540, as he passed through on his way to Flanders.

Marcelino Menéndez y Pelayo said of the play: "[The acts] have no ties to one another other than the fact that all make reference to the person of the Emperor, and it can even be said that only the first and second [*sic*] acts have any relationship to the title." He also claimed, "This piece, as can be seen, lacks any dramatic unity, and is no more than a chronicle in dialogue form . . . but it is well-written, it holds interest for the noble examples of valor and courtliness that it evokes, and there is no lack of amenity to be found in the episodic scenes with which it abounds."[10] Arnold G. Reichenberger agreed that the play was an episodic work centering about the Emperor, but he too failed to find any unifying theme. Reichenberger attempted to justify his acceptance of the play by pointing out the visual nature of the actions presented on stage and the stage directions that, more detailed in nature than is usual, indicate the "stately pageantry" that was meant to unfold before the eyes of the spectators.[11] Reichenberger, however, did not choose to follow up on the clue he provided as to the nature of the piece, that is the word he chose to describe what actually goes on when the piece is presented, "pageantry." *Charles V in France,* then, continues to be studied and criticized as one of Lope's dramatically weaker, relatively minor dramas on an historical theme.

Contrary to what Menéndez y Pelayo and Reichenberger reported, I find that there are, indeed, structural and thematic devices employed in the play that tend to unify the work, but which, nevertheless, leave it episodic and linear in structure. One action (not a true plot or even subplot) runs through all three acts of the play yet never reaches the level of importance that would enable an audience to identify it as anything but a minor aspect of the work as a whole: The story of Leonor and the *loco amor* (mad passion) she conceives for the Emperor. In Act I, she watches his entrance, falls in love with him at a distance, and swears to follow him until she can enjoy his loving embrace. In the second act, having followed Charles to Toledo, she attempts, through the good offices of Pacheco, to seduce the Emperor and is rejected. In the third act, her passion has driven her insane and her *locuras* (insane actions) become an entertainment for the court. Another aspect of the play, that serves to unify it, is the recurrent theme of the Emperor as the fountainhead of justice. In Act I, he deals out justice to the braggart soldier Pacheco, promoting him to aide when he defends the honor of the Emperor and the Spanish troops in a series of bar room brawls. In Act II, Charles again wields the rod of justice as he deals with the Duke of the Infantado. In the third act, Francis yields his royal power to Charles during the latter's stay in Paris, and Charles takes advantage of this courtesy to mete out justice once more to all who come before him. There can be no doubt that these elements all intertwine in a deliberate effort at artistic unification; since as each episode passes we find that it forms a mirror in which the actions and themes of preceding and following episodes are reflected, sometimes on an ideal, others on a mundane, plane.

The Tragedy of King Sebastian and the Baptism of the Prince of Morocco. Act I portrays events that lead to the disaster of Alcazarquivir and the death of King Sebastian of Portugal: the Portuguese King's refusal to accept the advice of his cousin Philip II, and the internecine strife in Morocco that brought on the overwhelming and unexpected attack by an army of Moors at the very moment when Sebastian was making peace with another group. The second act presents Muley Jeque in Andalusia as a guest of Philip after his expulsion from Africa by his cousin. He is present at the festival of Santa María de la Cabeza where he first shows an interest in the outer trappings of Christianity and then asks for instruction in the deeper mysteries of the religion. Act III deals with Muley's definitive conversion, an abortive assassination attempt plotted by his own retainers who would rather see him dead than Christian, and finally the pageantry of his baptism.

Menéndez y Pelayo, in dealing with the literary and artistic value of the work, said: "This play, with all its 56 characters, is indisputably one of the most irregular and disorderly that he (Lope) composed. It contains two completely unconnected actions." After describing the "monstrous nature of the structure," he went on to insist that, "In spite of the quite absurd plot, this dramatic poem contains partial beauties that make the reading of it tolerable."[12] No critic, until now, has cared to quarrel with this judgment. Thus, the work remains beneath the cloud of oblivion, visible only to those *lopistas* who insist on relishing every last bite of that poet's vast offering. Yet those partial beauties of which Menéndez y Pelayo spoke are not isolated in various episodes. They have a very close thematic interrelationship to each other and to the work as a whole. Sebastian's deeply religious convictions that force him to seek the conversion of the non-Christian world is reflected in the profound Christian feelings of the pilgrims in Andalusia as developed in the second act, a portrayal of local customs that called forth the highest praise from Menéndez y Pelayo. Civil War, that in Morocco leads to the death of Sebastian and the banishment of the young Muley Jeque, leads as well to the unification of Portugal and Spain. The comic contrast of Mohammedan and Christian marriage customs (brought to the stage in a scene between Muley Jeque and a feminine pilgrim while they observe the procession of Act II) leads directly to his instruction in the deeper mysteries of the faith in the third act, an act that is dominated by the pageantry of his baptism in the presence of the royal family and the ecclesiastical hierarchy of Spain. Each of these acts is dominated by the pageantry at its base: the arrival in Morocco of Sebastian and his troops and the battle of Alcazarquivir, the procession in honor of Santa María de la Cabeza, and the baptism of the Prince. Although the piece undoubtedly lacks plot (and the conflict and resolution of conflict that this implies), there is certainly present an entire series of unifying themes and processes.

Obviously anyone attempting to look at this play as drama is immediately baffled. There is no plot, no story line, no familiar structure to aid in perceiving what unity the work does have. This reflects the fact that the work was probably prepared as a pageant for an official occasion, perhaps for the official visit of Muley Jeque, baptized in 1593, to the royal court in 1602.[13] The work does not fail as historical pageantry, however. A seventeenth-century audience would have appreciated the vignettes of well-known personages pictured in interesting moments from recent history, the color and trapping of royal audiences, scenes from the battlefield, and picturesque religious celebrations, all mixed in and around a series of interesting and comic incidents from daily life, ballads celebrating real events, and especially, the titillating effect of sexually oriented material. Structurally the play is linear, one episode following the other with no attempt to build dramatic suspense, yet with the whole tied together by means of the two historically connected events with which it deals.

The Royal Reconciliation and Jewess of Toledo. The first act treats the youthful Alphonse VIII's siege of the castle of Zurita and the capture of Toledo through the treachery of Dominguillo. Alphonse, at the same time that he rewards the traitor with a pension, orders him blinded. Act II passes after an interlude of some years when Alphonse falls in love with Rachel, a Jewish girl, when he spies her bathing in the river. He takes Rachel as a mistress, thus alienating himself from Queen Leonor. Act III deals with the murder of Rachel seven years later by nobles worried over the state of the Kingdom. Alphonse and Leonor are reunited when she forgives him his infidelity.

James Castañeda, in his critical edition of the play, sums up the prevalent critical attitude toward this work, claiming that it "lacks the unity of texture and inspiration without which it could never be classified as one of Lope's best works."[14] Alexander A. Parker, after stating that "Both Lope and Tirso began by writing plays with no unity either of theme or plot, and both developed toward unification in and through the theme," comments further, "In Lope's *Las paces de los reyes y judía de Toledo,* both the main action and the theme are to be found only in the second and third acts."[15] The play has also been studied by David H. Darst and William C. McCrary.[16] Darst finds unity in the various life stages of the King: Act I deals with his childhood and adolescence, Act II with his youth, and Act III with his real manhood. These stages Darst relates to the pattern of the universal hero. McCrary carries Darst's conception of the play a step further, seeking to show that "The action which the plot of *Las paces* dramatizes . . . is essentially an extended rite of passage." Thus, both these critics see the unity of the play in historical theme rather than in dramatic conflict. In a recent paper presented to the Central Renaissance Conference, David Gitlitz quarreled with the generally negative evaluation of the work, finding that the few thematic connections reported by E. M. Wilson and Duncan Moir were not the only literary glue that held the piece together. Gitlitz found that the fundamental unity of this work, like that of many others, was to be found in the least dramatic of its elements, the language and the poetic images expressed through it.[17]

In *The Royal Reconciliation,* the images associated with fire, water, and blood form the main elements of the supporting imagistic structure. Fire is, at first, the erotic passion that inflames Alphonse: after

Rachel's death, it becomes rage directed at her assassins. Water is related to Alphonse's duties toward his kingdom but also, making use of the pastoral tradition, appears in connection with eroticism. Blood is tied to the wartime responsibilities of Alphonse and then becomes linked with the "bad blood" of the Jewess as well as the blood lust of vengeance. At the end, fire is transformed into the flame of divine love, water becomes the fountain of grace, and blood is transmuted into the love of the Virgin Mary. Unfortunately, one cannot create drama, real drama, through the use of imagery. In this very fact lies a clue to the solution I propose for the critical problem.

Looking back at the three plays we have been dealing with, we find, interestingly, that there is no dramatic conflict in any one of them, and in one case (*The Tragedy of King Sebastian*) there is not even an identifiable protagonist since Sebastian dies at the end of the first act and the Prince whose conversion and baptism is the topic of the other two acts is but a child at the time of the events of the first act. To some extent the same criticism may be made of *The Royal Reconciliation* since Alphonse VIII is shown at such widely differing stages of life in the first and in the other two acts. Darst goes so far as to state, "Significantly, *all* [my emphasis] the characters of Act I are retired and replaced by an entirely new cast."[18]

Rather than conflict, we find that the study about which the play on Charles V is built is thematic: the Emperor as the source of justice, the Church as the source of peace between neighboring countries. Indeed, this is precisely the message of the final scene of the third act: as Charles dispenses worldly reward in the Court at Paris, a set scene (*apariencia*) is unveiled showing, by means of allegorical figures, France and Spain in a loving embrace being blessed by the Pope. *The Tragedy of King Sebastian* uses every scene, every episode, to point to the blessing that would result from a universal acceptance of the Christian faith. Each episode, even those of the anomalous first act, point toward the ultimate conversion and baptism of the Moroccan prince. *The Royal Reconciliation*, a work the theme of which has furnished material for many a fine drama (Mira de Amescua's *La desgraciada Raquel* [The Unfortunate Rachel] and Grillparzer's *Die Judin von Toledo* [The Jewess of Toledo], etc.), centers about the naturation process of Alphonse VIII or the poetic imagery involved rather than any one of the many possible dramatic conflicts: love for a Jewish mistress, jealousy of the estranged Queen, the monarch's duty to state and people.

I submit that rather than criticize these three plays (and by extension a considerable number of other Golden Age *comedias*) as poorly constructed dramas, we should approach them first from the point of view of what they truly represent. If we do so, we find that they are admirably constructed, well-written, and artistically unified plays or, as in some cases, pageantry. Lope carefully utilized his thematic materials (political in the case of *Charles V,* religious in *The Tragedy,* and imagistic in *The Royal Reconciliation*) in order to maximize the desired appeal to the emotional loyalties or contemporary interests of the intended audience. The criticism of such works as poorly structured or badly written drama is erroneous at its base. They are not drama and, therefore, cannot be properly criticized for a failure to meet the standards of that literary vehicle.

Elements Relating to Dramatic Structures

The *comedia* is made up of a host of elements, some of which are embedded in the basic structures discussed above, others are used to flesh out the skeletal lines in order to make the whole pleasing to its audience, whether that audience be an active one, as when reading the work as a piece of literature, or a more passive one, as when the work is played before the public.[19] These elements include (1) the specific materials making up what we usually refer to as the details of plot and subplot, (2) the particular dramatic techniques used in presenting the materials, and (3) the different decorative elements typifying the style or language of the play.

Plot, Subplot, and the Triple Axis. The problems of the interrelationship of plot (the traditionally accepted basis for classifying the *comedia*), subplot, and the structure of the work are difficult though important to solve. The complications result from the manner in which a dramatist may choose to build a work from a mixture of source materials as he constructs each particular amalgam of plot and subplot. An additional problem becomes apparent when one attempts to resolve the fuzziness of the dividing lines that separate the areas of classification, a lack of definition caused, at least in part, by an author's desire to create an ambience of verisimilitude as he seeks poetic rather than historical truth.[20] Mira de Amescua's *La casa del tahur* [Gambler's Home], for example, is a play in which the author has overlaid the typical "Cape and sword" plot on a biblical base, the prodigal son story.[21] The same author has used a historical base for his *No hay dicha ni desdicha hasta la muerte* [There is Neither Fortune nor Misfortune until Death]; but in it he treats history in a cavalier fashion nearly destroying the facts as he invents motives, unites people from different centuries in the same action, and expands upon the legendary characteristics of the people with whom he deals, all in a search for poetic truth.[22] Combining much of the same historical material used by Mira with a well-developed comedy of character *(comedia de figurón)*, Juan Ruiz de Alarcón in his play *Don Domingo de Don Blas*[23] uses the history to support the "truth" of his characters in an opposite manner. Mira uses the figures from the past to put aesthetic distance between his audience and the philosophical and moral lesson he wishes to approach. Alarcón uses the source material to lend an air of truth to the fantastic character he is presenting.

Can we properly classify a *comedia* that, to a great extent, is "cape and sword" drama as biblical just because the author chooses the prodigal son story upon which to base his main plot? Yet, is the play properly classified if we ignore that base? Is Mira's *There Is Neither Fortune* an historical play in spite of the anachronistic presence of characters who lived a century apart? Is Alarcón's *Don Domingo* a character study, or is it a historical play, in view of the fact that the characters exist only within the historical ambience he presents? No one has as yet come up with a final, satisfactory answer for such questions; however, perhaps Lope himself suggested a means of approaching the problem when he described all *comedias* as being based either on historical materials *tragedias)*, on invented stories *(comedias)*, or on both *(tragicomedias)*.[24]

One of the axes upon which any given *comedia* can be located for the purposes of classification is the vector stemming from characters and events taken from history or legend. It passes through the realm of historic fact, includes material from folk tales and reaches toward the world of the novelistic. From this line any character or event may be plucked around which to design a plot. A second axis, that which concerns the period represented, is easily identified. It runs from the distant past, either biblical or classical, through the medieval past, to the present time, which was, for the purposes of those who wrote *comedias,* the period covered by the sixteenth and seventeenth centuries. A third axis, more difficult to perceive, perhaps, indicates the philosophical thrust of the work—the point of view from which the dramatist attacks his play. Perhaps this is even better expressed (in fact, the "new critic" would insist upon attacking it thus) as the point of view perceived by the audience. That is, the place at which the given work can be located on a line dividing the didactic from the delightful, the *deleitar aprovechando* that so preoccupied both writers and critics of the period. There are, of course, other axes that might be used to describe or classify a *comedia* more exactly; however, just as we find that three dimensions are sufficient for all practical purposes in the work-a-day world and leave the theoretically possible fourth and higher dimensions to those mathematicians willing to deal with them on their own terms, we can get by in the world of the *comedia* with the three just described. It is clear that any classification system attempting to group *comedias* by reference to only one or two of the qualities upon which they depend is certain to lead to misunderstanding or inexactitude. In discussing the works of the minor dramatists with whom this book deals, I will make an effort to demonstrate how they can be classified by means of this system as I discuss the intersection of plot and structure found in the works.

   Dramatic Techniques.   It is not just plot and structure that meet to form a *comedia.* The dramatist makes use of a variety of techniques as he develops his work. Some, if the genre were the novel, could be referred to as narrative techniques. These have to do with the ways in which the author combines plot and subplot relating them to the overall structure, as well as the manner in which he uses dramatic irony, foreshadowing, and other such tools in order to increase awareness on the part of his audience of the play's reason for being. In the early years of the seventeenth century when the playwrights were still learning to handle their materials, multiple subplots were often used as the prime means for redirecting the attention of the audience and to increase the suspense called for in Lope's *New Art of Writing Comedias.* Gradually the subplots were reduced in number and strength as the poets learned to use other means for achieving the same purpose. For example, Mira de Amescua in *La rueda de la Fortuna* [The Wheel of Fortune], a play written prior to 1604, depends almost completely on the multiple subplots to block the ultimate resolution of his main plot from the audience's view until it is presented on stage. The result has been general condemnation of the work by modern critics as a disorderly work in which too much appears to be happening.[25]

The main plot of *The Wheel of Fortune* deals with the rise of Heraclius, the true son of the Emperor Mauritius, to the throne of the Eastern Roman Empire through his own valor, and his marriage to the beautiful captive Mitilene. The three points that define the trajectory of the protagonist are his arrival at court with Heraclianus, his surrogate father *(in)*; his gentle treatment of Mitilene when he encounters the ladies of the court in the mountains where they are hiding from the revolution that overthrew the tyrant Mauritius *(pp)*; and his acceptance of her hand in marriage when he is elected to succeed the wicked Phocus, murderer of Mauritius *(ec)*. This plot is so nearly hidden behind a wealth of subplots that it is difficult to perceive.

Menéndez y Pelayo led the way for modern critical judgment of the work when he wrote that there was enough dramatic material in *The Wheel of Fortune* to construct many plays.[26] Mira presents us with (1) the rise and fall of the general Leontius in balanced counterposition to that of the general Philip, (2) the stratagems of the Empress to obtain her husband's help for the beleaguered Papal states, (3) the love for the captive Princess Mitilene on the part of the false Prince Theodosius, by Mauritius himself, as well as the two generals, (4) the unrequited love of Princess Theodora for Leontius, and (5) the plots of Phocus to murder Mauritius and take the throne for himself. Wheels within wheels! While in the course of the play, the wheel upon which Heraclius sits makes one half-turn lifting him from nothingness to ruling position, Leontius and Philip each go one full circle, and the other plots seem to be on even smaller, more rapidly moving hubs that in turn support the major machinery. At any moment in the play, we encounter several individuals, each at one of the four cardinal points on Fortune's wheel. There is certainly sufficient action in the work to keep an audience's attention. The true marvel is that Mira created a successful, thematically unified work instead of chaos out of the massive amount of material he employed.

By the year 1616 when he wrote *Gambler's Home,* Mira had learned to handle the problems of unity and suspense without such heavy dependence on subplot. In that play he superimposes one plot (the widow who gets herself a wealthy husband) on another (the prodigal son who reforms and returns to the welcoming arms of wife and father). Obviously recognizing the difficulties inherent in maintaining suspense and interest in such an easily recognized story as that of the prodigal son, Mira uses it instead as a source for foreshadowing, dramatic irony, and the special voices from heaven *(voces del cielo)* technique for which he is well known. He uses these techniques in the one plot to act upon the other in a way that maintains our interest and heightens suspense.[27]

Mira's later plays show a still greater refinement of these same techniques.[28] The plot and subplot relationships become so unified, each element so interdependent, that one cannot easily be separated from the other; and the dramatist uses, instead, the elements of foreshadowing, omen, irony, and the typical technique of deceiving with the truth *(engañar con la verdad)* to achieve his purposes. The gradual mastery of these tricks of the trade by Mira is, to a great extent, identical with their fortune among the minor dramatists of the period since these naturally tended to be imitators rather than initiators in their field of endeavor. Even when a lesser dramatist did initiate a practice, it was often as a reaction to an already too well established practice, a dramatic cliché, rather than as a move in a completely new direction.

Many such technical elements, as the *comedia* developed into the stagnated art form it became during the latter half of the seventeenth century, took on the nature of dramatic conventions. Later dramatists often felt constrained to comment on their use of such devices with statements like "What a thing to happen in a *comedia,* like those of twenty years ago!" or "Those young people so proud of their experience, will figure that this is a *comedia.*"[29] Sometimes they did this as a warning of their own awareness of the triteness of the situation, or so that the audience might be prepared for a different outcome; more often the technique was used to economize by avoiding a longer, more complete development of the action so indicated.

Decorative Elements. Before entering upon the body of the present text, there remain some aspects of technique as related to structure that need to be discussed: The stylistic devices that were often employed with a special relationship to the basic plot structure. Such rhetorical devices include the use of *sententiae,* proverbs, classical and other allusions, iconographical materials, fables or short tales, and the polymetry that was the basic stylistic vehicle for the *comedia.*

Lope, in the *New Art of Writing Comedias,* refers to the use of *sententiae* as a means of educating and delighting the audience as well as decorating the language of the play. A popular saying or proverb, besides serving as a source for titles, was often used in the same way. I know of no existing study that treats of the relationship of these to dramatic structure, yet such could undoubtedly be shown just as it could for the frequent allusions to biblical, classical, and folkloric characters and events.[30] For example, one such instance is evident in the reference to the Antiochus-Seleucus story at a key moment of dramatic interest in Lope's *El castigo sin venganza* [Punishment without Vengeance] the moment when Casandra and Federico finally give in to their mutual passion and go to bed together. The correlations among allusions, references, *sententiae,* and the structures previously indicated as major elements of the drama are too frequent for that to have been accidental.

In the same way the relationship between Renaissance iconography and dramatic structure needs more study. James F. Burke showed in a recent study, for example, how Alarcón used the emblematic image of Truth to ensure that the audience realized the meaning of his *La verdad sospechosa* [Truth Suspect] by using that image to underscore key moments in the play.[31] Calderón's use of both horse and light imagery in his *La vida es sueño* [Life Is a Dream] at the key moments in the structure of that work, moments heralded by the meetings of Rosaura and Segismundo, certainly falls within the pattern and has been studied previously.[32] Related to such iconographical elements, but as yet relatively unstudied, is the way in which authors employed contemporary or classical cosmology to the same end. For example, Mira de Amescua in *The Wheel of Fortune* (presenting yet another in the series of wheel images, as Edward Hopper has shown in a recent doctoral dissertation)[33] makes the jealous Princess Theodora spread her cape and move in a circle between the static Mitilene and the ecstatic Leontius who, trying to glimpse the beauty of the captive Princess despite Theodora's efforts to hide her from him, moves in his own circular path. Throughout this scene Mira makes constant references to the relative positions within the cosmos of the Sun (Mitilene), the Moon (Theodora), and to the eclipses that result from their movements with relation to each other and to the Earth (Leontius).

Mira, as I have shown, elsewhere used short stories *(fabulillas, cuentecillos)* as a means of pointing out critical moments in the structure of some of his plays.[34] Other seventeenth-century dramatists used the same technique. Lope de Vega, for example, in his *Punishment without Vengeance,* points to the meeting of the young Federico with his stepmother-to-be (the initiating incident of this tragedy) through a story in which the almost commonplace horse-sex imagery is employed to explain the situation, comparing his father to a white stallion frightened into submission and good behavior by a lion (the stepmother or even, perhaps, a foreshadowing of the role the Pope and the Church will play in the Duke's moral rehabilitation). Similar imagery is repeatedly usd at key moments throughout the play.[35]

Critics, especially non-Hispanists, have often wondered about the purposes served by the polymetry typical of the *comedia.* In a recent study I have shown how at least one of the purposes behind the use of polymetry lay in its relationship to the structure of the work.[36] Besides serving the already recognized purposes of lending a distinctive quality to the various types of scenes (narrative passages, love plaints, or soliloquies), and acting as an additional means for audibly separating the scenes and varied locales one from another, a strophic form came to carry some of the structural burden of the *comedia.* Just as it became almost a requirement of the genre that each act end with a *laisse* of octosyllabic verse with assonant rhyme in alternate lines *(romance)* to signal the impending close *(dt),* the poet-author often used an unusual or distinctive strophic form (sometimes a set-piece of poetry or, in later plays, a musical piece) to call the attention of the audience to important moments in the drama.

The chapters that follow here will attempt to deal chronologically, in general, with some of the most outstanding of the minor dramatists of the Golden Age, and to show how each made use of the elements and techniques defined here that had been developed principally by the major dramatic poets of the time, those who set the pattern for the developing *comedia.*

As the popularity of the genre developed during the seventeenth century and as the techniques of writing in that form became better understood, more and more poets and would-be poets joined the ranks of those writing *comedias*. Therefore, although in the next chapter, dealing with the earliest followers of Lope de Vega, I am able to write about nearly seventy-five per cent of the extant theatrical production of the period (I omit only those poets who could be best classed as belonging to the "also-ran" category), the list of those not included in the main study grows larger with each succeeding era. The choice is a personal one made after wide reading among the extant works of seventeenth-century poets and should not be taken to mean that only those included here wrote plays worthy of study or made lasting contributions to the development of the genre. The field of the *comedia* is all but inexhaustible.

Chapter Two
The Earliest *Lopistas* (1601–1620)

The usual division of Golden Age dramatists into those that belong to the so-called Lopean cycle and those of the Calderonian school will be here so subdivided as to distinguish the earliest *Lopistas* who wrote mainly before 1621 from those who followed. The choice of this date is based on at least three sets of facts: (1) the political changes that came to a head in that year (the Duke of Lerma, favorite of Philip III, had been dismissed in 1618 and the resulting political vacuum was not truly filled until that King had died and Philip IV came to the throne early in 1621. With the succession, the real power was assumed by the new King's favorite, the Duke of Olivares); (2) the political changes were reflected not only in conditions pertaining to the theater but in a whole set of social conditions and customs that became a center of interest for the dramatists of the period;[1] (3) at about the same time, the plays that were being written by Lope de Vega suffered a decrease in popularity as the public came to demand newer and different styles of writing, a new style that Lope himself was forced to accept and master in the years before his death.[2]

Besides Lope de Vega, the minor figures treated here, and the writers of the Valencian school of dramatists,[3] three major playwrights produced many of their plays in the years 1601–1620: Guillén de Castro y Belvis, Antonio Mira de Amescua, and Gabriel Téllez (Tirso de Molina).[4] These three, together with some of the younger dramatists who were to dominate the post-Lopean period, were the really popular writers of the decade 1621–1630 even though the public never completely forgot its adulation of Lope. Castro, Mira, and Tirso, however, all wrote a large number of plays in the period before 1621. These earlier plays, in general, reflect even more closely than do their later works, the power of the genius who first learned to manage the threads from which the *comedia* was woven. We must, then, keep in mind, as we proceed, that the figures discussed here form but a minor appendage to a much more important body of writers and works from the same period.

Miguel Sánchez

In his *Laurel de Apolo* (the critico-epic poem written in 1628–1630 in praise of contemporary writers), Lope de Vega cites Miguel Sánchez, the Divine *(el divino)*, as a predecessor who had died in Plasencia.[5] Sánchez has left the texts of three extant plays, one of them still unpublished. Other than this, little is known for certain or can even be deduced about him or his life. Because of long-standing confusion as to whether the poet's name was Miguel or Juan Sánchez, we really know even less than the usual sources tell us about him. It is possible, however, to be fairly sure about a few facts: he was an ecclesiastic who served for a time as secretary to the Bishop of Cuenca, he wrote the three *comedias* that remain to us before the year 1612, probably in the period 1595–1610, and he died before 1630.

Agustín de Rojas Villandrando names Miguel Sánchez as one of the poets writing *comedias* in 1602, describing his verse as witty, wise, and sententious.[6] In the *New Art of Writing Comedias* (1609), Lope de Vega mentions Sánchez's ability to manage the technique of deceiving with the truth *(engañar con la verdad)*. In fact, he claims that Miguel Sánchez invented the process.[7] Miguel Cervantes, in his *Viaje del Parnaso* [Voyage to Parnassus] of 1615, cited him as a writer worthy of joining the ranks of the good poets.[8] Lope again mentions Sánchez with praise in his *Filomena* of 1621,[9] as well as in the later text cited above. Besides the three *comedias* by Miguel Sánchez, we have at least two poetic pieces by him that were printed in 1604–1605.[10] All of this points to Miguel Sánchez as a writer of some importance during the period that interests us here.

It is possible to trace a series of misunderstandings and misquotations concerning Sánchez that leads directly from Agustín Durán, through Alberto Lista, Ramón de Mesonero Romanos, Cayetano de la Barrera, and Julián Paz y Melia to all later literary historians. These have complicated the problem of identification; however, it is clear, contrary to what these critics reported, that Miguel and Juan Sánchez were two people. The proof of this lies in a comparison of the two manuscripts of the play *Cerco y toma de Túnez y la Goleta por el Emperador Carlos Quinto*[11] [The Siege and Taking of Tunis and La Goleta by the Emperor Charles the Fifth], attributed to Miguel Sánchez, and the text of a play with the same title attributed to Juan Sánchez in the volume of

Doze comedias de varios autores [Twelve Comedias by Various Authors], published in Tortosa by Francisco Martorell in 1638. Besides the *princeps* of Miguel Sánchez's *La isla bárbara* [The Barbaric Isle], that volume contains a sequel to the other play by Juan Sánchez with the title *Segunda parte del cosario Barbaroja y huérfano desterrado* [The Second Part of the Corsair Barbarossa and the Orphan Banished]. This suggests that the title originally given to the first play in that volume by Juan Sánchez was not that by which it was generally known. It is, indeed, better described as a play about Barbarossa than about Charles the Fifth.[12]

Most, if not all, modern criticism of Miguel Sánchez can be traced to two nineteenth-century evaluations of his work. Seemingly basing his criticism of the poet's plays on what Alberto Lista had had to say about one of them, Mesonero Romanos included the *comedia La guarda cuidadosa* [The Careful Guard] in the first of the two volumes of texts he devoted to Lope's contemporaries.[13] Lista, as quoted there, spoke of the rather full gamut of poetic imagery to be found in *The Careful Guard* and the author's ability to make a plot grow out of the initial incident. Lista had concluded his article by describing Sánchez's theater as a link between Lopean and Calderonian drama. This is the only one of his conclusions with which Mesonero Romanos quarrels. He points out the chronological absurdity of that evaluation.

Hugo A. Rennert, who is responsible for the only modern editions of *The Careful Guard* and *The Barbaric Isle,*[14] noting that Lope had described Sánchez as the inventor of the technique of deceiving with the truth, remarks that he does not find it used in either of the two plays he edited.[15] It seems probable, however, that Rennert saw in that reference to the procedure something other than what Lope had intended, because, as we will see, one of the most noteworthy elements of the author's technique in these two plays is precisely his use of dramatic irony, evidently the aspect to which Lope refers. Rennert, like the earlier critics who dealt with Sánchez, prefers *The Careful Guard* to *The Barbaric Isle,* but he insists that both plays are in a Lopean style.

The Siege and Taking of Tunis and La Goleta by the Emperor Charles the Fifth.[16] Unlike the dramatic monstrosities written by Juan Sánchez and often confused with his plays, Miguel Sánchez's unedited *Siege and Taking of Tunis* is a rather well worked out and unified historical pageant, linear in structure, whose prime reason for being is to praise Charles V. Differing from the plays by Juan Sánchez, the role of Barbarossa is here reduced to the minimum necessary to contrast with the character of Charles. The play resolves itself into a series of royal audiences, parades and processions, and minor incidents that show the faith, generosity, valor, continence, justice, and wisdom of the Emperor. Barbarossa is shown, in contrast, to be superstitious, evil, unjust, and sly. Two of the many scenes are especially well presented and deserve mention. One, at the midpoint of the play, is a dream sequence in which Charles V sees Christ on a Cross leading him and the Church to victory. Alongside the Cross are the Pillars of Hercules joined by a device carrying the motto *Plus Ultra* to indicate the power of Spanish hegemony. The other is a comic scene in which Charles's action in choosing water as a beverage is contrasted with that of his drunken German troops. The work, like many others of the same nature, has a practically limitless cast of characters who appear in a linear series of episodes designed to delight the eye as well as the ear. Sánchez's versification is smooth and keenly honed, and, if scribal errors were eliminated, would be quite correct. He makes free use of figurative language and even in this early play (written before 1598 as is shown by reference to Philip II as reigning monarch) the *sententiae* appear regularly and frequently. Sánchez uses only four different strophes in the play, thus showing a tendency to avoid frequent changes of verse form. He uses *octavas* (the strophe typically used in epic poems) for those scenes in which Charles V is being praised in words rather than in action; *romances* (ballad meter) are employed in the narrative passages that explain off-stage action; *sueltos* (blank verse) are used for the scene in which the drunken soldiers appear; and the balance of the work is written in *quintillas* (a five-line, octosyllabic strophe). This lack of interest in strophic variety appears in his two later plays as well.

The Careful Guard. [17]   The better of the two dramatically structured *comedias* we have from the hand of Miguel Sánchez, *The Careful Guard,* merits more sustained attention than we will be able to give the other as an example of what one minor dramatist was able to accomplish in the first decade of the seventeenth century.

Act I. Nisea has been brought by her father, Leucato, to their country home in order to break up an incipient love affair *(ex)*. The

Prince comes hunting and decides that Nisea is fairer game than the deer he was pursuing *(in)*. Her maid Arsinda is glad that a new suitor, one that can pay for her aid, has come to take Nisea's mind off Florencio *(ex)*. This gallant is brought into the house unconscious, having fallen from his horse not far from the country home to which he had traced her *(ra)*. He recovers but is badly hurt and his head is bandaged so that when the Prince sneaks back from the hunt to pursue Nisea, he finds Florencio in the house but cannot identify him. The two, though polite, immediately distrust each other *(ra)*. Because she is sure that Florencio's head wounds will kill him if they are not properly tended to, Nisea is upset when he, at the Prince's urging, leaves to spend the night elsewhere *(ra)*.

Act II. Florencio appears in a guard's uniform. After recovering sufficiently, he has taken employment as a game warden on the preserve and, deliberately having led everyone to think him dead as a result of his wounds, is taking advantage of the position he is in to watch and learn about Nisea's true feelings *(ra)*. Even though no one else can recognize him since they had only seen him with bandaged face and head, Nisea immediately recognizes him when she finds him alone in the woods. After a short scene of recrimination and forgiveness *(ra)*, she decides that she would like to go hunting and use his services as guide and "gun"-bearer *(pp)*. Deliberately sensuous figurative language is used at this point to emphasize the situation. No doubt is left in the mind of the audience about what is really going on. Ridding themselves of their companions, they say:

ARIADENO: Whoever has anything to guard had better do so.
                          (He leaves)
NISEA: I'm going off down towards that valley. Is that gun of yours good for anything?
FLORENCIO: Reasonably so.
NISEA: I'll try it out. Florencio, at last I've found you. I wonder if my soul still holds yours.
                     I thought so at the beginning,
                     but now I can't believe it.
                     Lay your half on my breast
                     so that I may be informed. . . . (15a)

The Prince decides to spend the night at the woodcutter's cottage in order to be near enough to visit Nisea that same evening *(pt)*. Florencio and the Prince meet in the garden. Florencio, made increasingly jealous by the Prince's presence, explains that he is only carrying out his duties as a guard *(pt)*. He goes off as ordered and meets the woodcutter's daughter Florela who has had to give up her own bed so that the Prince might have it. Florencio watches over her so that she can rest in safety *(rt)*.

Act III. Everyone is out hunting. Nisea is pursued by the Prince, he by Florencio *(pt)*. Florencio and Nisea meet and exchange lovers' complaints *(rt)*. When the Prince faces Nisea, it is only to be insulted by her as she rejects him, insisting that what he has in mind is her dishonor and that if he were the kind of Prince he should be, she should not have to fight him off *(rt)*. Florencio returns in the company of the woodcutter Sileno, who complains to the Prince that Florencio, while spending the night with her, has attempted to rape his daughter. Florencio is arrested by the Prince as much to get him out of the way as to appease Sileno *(pt)*. The Prince, seeking a means to avenge himself on Nisea for having rebuffed him, decides that he will arrange for her to fall in love with a commoner in the disguise of a noble, thus punishing her as suits the crime. Ariadeno, servant to Florencio, who had been employed by the Prince after his master's "death," offers to talk his friend the "careful guard" into making love to Nisea pretending to be the gentleman Florencio in disguise *(rt)*. Leucato, as a result of finding Florencio and Nisea together, believes that the Prince has been lingering in the neighborhood only to serve as a go-between for Florencio. He then insists on an immediate marriage *(ec)*. The Prince is at first shocked at the lengths to which his prank has driven the others *(re)*. At last he is satisfied as the truth comes out and those who know the facts about his machinations promise to keep the secret thus allowing him to save face *(dt)*.

The play is easily classified as a novelistic work of Italianate stamp, set in a period contemporary to its composition, and clearly intended to entertain even though a thesis (that what seems bad often eventually turns out to be good) is suggested throughout. Interestingly, the thesis is first set forth in the *Loa* that, since the earliest printing of the work, has been attached to it.

With limited success, the play follows the pattern we have suggested here as basic to drama in the *comedia.* It holds one's interest up to the mid-point in spite of a rather ill-defined initiating incident. That beginning is not well marked because these are two points from which the plot seems to spring and develop: the arrival of the Prince, and Florencio's fall from his horse. In part because of this structurally weak base (Nisea is the only character common to both incidents), and in part because Nisea, as protagonist, is the real center of the play, the plot loses suspense when she gives in sexually at the middle of the second act. The basic weakness of the work, however, is found in the fact that the author creates conflict in the people and events that surround Nisea but never within her own feelings or actions. She has known and loved Florencio before the play begins, she never doubts his love for her, and she is the sexual aggressor at the moment of dramatic climax, the pivotal point of the play. The sporadic conflicts that do develop around Nisea are not sufficient to create drama where none exists.

Nor is the pivotal point well marked. The sexual joining of Florencio and Nisea in the middle of the second act is the point at which the lady's future is determined. By rule of convention, she must marry Florencio. Yet there is a lack of warmth in the treatment of the incident. The author neglects to do more than indicate that important action by means of suggestive imagery. In actual performance of the play, actions would certainly be used to reinforce the meaning of the hunt imagery employed when the couple goes off into the woods unaccompanied. Indeed, those actions themselves could possibly create the needed climax. Following this point in the play, Sánchez seems to have had trouble bringing the story to an end. Unnecessary and extraneous material such as the problem with the woodcutter's daughter and other such false leads are rather fully developed in Sánchez's attempts to maintain the needed suspense. As a result, the emotional response one should feel as the play approaches resolution never arrives. Instead the *comedia* bogs down in an overlong series of episodes only marginally related to the plot.

There are areas, however, in which Sánchez does excel. These rescue the play and separate it from the mass of dramatically weak texts by other minor dramatists that we have at hand. These are the qualities for which Sánchez was praised by his own contemporaries: the *sententiae* that spice his verse, the lyric flow of his poetry, the mastery of the imagery that he employs, and the ability to handle dramatic irony (*engañar con la verdad*) as a theatrical technique.

Sánchez's verse is alive with the pointed didactic phrases or *sententiae*, frequently dependent upon a conceit, that were so appreciated at the time. He also manages well the various poetic techniques typical of cultured poetry. Recapitulation of images and parallel structuralization are the most easily recognized. For example, when the Prince first approaches Nisea, he swears to be faithful in his love for her. He hopes, if he fails to honor his promise, that he may die torn to pieces by a fierce bear, wounded by a traitor's sword, hurt in a fall from his horse, or poisoned by a viper's bite. Sánchez devotes one stanza to each of the elements in this series, identifying with it a characteristic quality of failing love. In her reply Nisea briefly recapitulates, reminding him that there are no bears, traitors, horses, or vipers present to witness his vows.

Besides the constantly present *hunt-love* image already mentioned, the play maintains much other sexual imagery. Among the most noteworthy is the *sex-fire* relationship that is consistently related to the woodcutter's daughter. When Florela first offers to care for Florencio at her father's cottage, she mentions the drink, food, warmth, and fire to be found there. In spite of his refusal of this offer, she repeats her approach after having escaped from the taunting of the Prince's men. Florencio remains constant to his love for Nisea even as he watches over the girl's repose, and Florela—comparing him to the forested mountain—warns him of the danger he runs by remaining in such close proximity to the flames of love that she feels.

In addition, Sánchez uses the less common image of *sex-storytelling*. Florencio, after spending the afternoon alone with Nisea out in the woods, comes to her balcony that night and offers to tell her some more tales of the same nature as those with which he had entertained her that afternoon. Nisea wonders at his capacity for "storytelling" while the eavesdropping Florela, in an aside, remarks that she would certainly like to hear some of those tales. Thus, through his imagery, the author creates an openly sensuous atmosphere sure to please his audience.

Although throughout *The Careful Guard* Sánchez makes use of the technique of deceiving with the truth, the most sustained use of that procedure is found in the third act. Dramatic irony is inherent to the situation that develops when the Prince, believing Florencio to be a common deserter who has accepted employment as a forest guard (to avoid being brought to military justice), hires him to make love (in disguise) to Nisea. Florencio accepts the proposal and thereupon assumes his true identity. The audience, fully aware of the double deception, is delighted by the constant use of speeches and situations of multiple meaning that depend upon the supposed state of knowledge or relative ignorance of the various characters on stage. As many as four different levels of irony are present at any given moment.

In so far as strophic changes are concerned, *The Careful Guard,* like the *Siege and Taking of Tunis,* is relatively simple. It is written principally in *redondillas* (stanzas of four octosyllabic verses rhyming *abba* in consonance), the strophic form that was replacing *quintillas* as the basic vehicle for drama by the first decade of the seventeenth century. There are three short passages of *sueltos,* one each of *tercetos* ("tiercets") and *romance,* as well as three sonnets.

The Barbaric Isle. The same simple pattern of verse usage is found in the third play by Sánchez, one that has a reliable *ad quem* date of 1611. That play, too, is written in *redondillas,* with one passage each of *octavas, sueltos,* and a sonnet. This simplicity of strophic arrangement is noteworthy, but not altogether unusual in that period, a time when Guillén de Castro and Lope de Vega were experimenting with the *redondilla* as the only strophic form for the *comedia.*[18]

The Barbaric Isle is an interesting novelistic play (most easily read in Rennert's edition), contemporary in time, with clear didactic intent. Sánchez, rather than limit the work to one unified thesis, vacillates between two. Thus, to some extent he weakens the force of the play. Both theses are present throughout the play; however, his insistent pointing to the fact that too large a dose of truth can get one into trouble dominates the first half of the *comedia.* In the second half, Sánchez seems to be just as interested in demonstrating that a ruler must use his powers with moderation and to an end other than his own personal pleasure.

Act I. King Normando, of an unnamed country, is in love with a lady of the court, Nísida, who is secretly maried to Emilio. Emilio has been banished from court, but Nísida's brother Vitelio is present to protect her *(ex)*. Artfully making use of iconography (in the emblem books of the period, Truth is often represented as a nude woman battling the forces of Time), Sánchez presents his first thesis in the initiating incident of the play. The King, plotting to rid himself of the main barrier preventing his free access to the favors of Nísida, pretends to test the courtesy of her courtier brother by allowing a letter he has been reading to be blown overboard. Vitelio jumps into the sea to rescue the letter and return it to the King, who refuses to have the ship turned in order that Vitelio can get back aboard. His excuse is that the sea is too dangerous and he does not wish to endanger another life. At this misdeed, the powers that be raise a furious storm and the King is forced to seek shelter on land at the Barbaric Isle. Vitelio, who has been able to divest himself of his clothing in order to swim, arrives and faces the King. Angry at the double treason (he is fully aware of what the King has done and why), Vitelio insists that since he is physically naked he will speak the bare truth *(in)*. The King uses this discourtesy as an excuse for marooning Vitelio on the island, which is inhabited by barbarian tribes *(ra)*.

Act II. Vitelio shows that he has learned his lesson to some extent when he prevaricates in order to rescue the barbarian Princess Troyla from the machinations of the Barbarian King, her brother, who has usurped the throne *(ra)*. The last of King Normando's opponents is finally banished and all of them, by one means or another, end up on the same island *(ra)*. The dramatic climax of the play arrives when the Queen, jealous of her husband and interested in insuring her own position, orders Nísida killed *(pp)*. Rather than carry out this foul deed, the master-at-arms abandons Nísida, too, on the coast of the island *(rt)*. The King, aware of the truth and still in search of his own pleasure, follows Nísida to the island accompanied by Emilio, her husband *(pt)*. The Queen follows the King *(rt)*, and the father of Nísida and Vitelio, trying to trace what has happened to his children, follows her *(rt)*. Sánchez's use of the truth-deception opposition comes to the fore again in his presentation of how Vitelio again gets into difficulties when he truthfully introduces Nísida to the Princess Troyla as his sister *(pt)*, and Emilio (like the biblical Abraham) saves himself by untruthfully introducing her as *his* sister to the Barbarian usurper *(rt)*.

Act III. As was the case in *The Careful Guard*, the third act of *The Barbaric Isle* is marred by an overlong series of episodes and false leads that only delay the conclusion of the play rather than increase dramatic tension as the end approaches. Sánchez does not seem to have realized that the necessary tension is created by means of opposing the potential and the real trajectories of the protagonist. He attempts, instead, to create suspense by opposing episodes dealing with the minor characters to the trajectory of the main plot. In spite of this, the play is another example of his ability to write pleasing verse-drama dotted with *sententiae* and the other literary and rhetorical figures that were the fashion of the time. Just as evident here is his interest in the technique of deceiving with the truth as a means of presenting a dramatically ironic plot. The truth-deception paradox is the stuff from which this play is made.

Damián Salucio del Poyo

Born in Murcia, probably about 1550, a date suggested by that of his marriage to Doña Beatriz de Avalos Lara y Soto in 1574, Damián Salucio del Poyo became a resident of Seville, where he died in 1614. The descendant of a wealthy Genoese (Saluzzio was the original name), who had married into the Murcian *hidalguía* (minor nobility), he was financially secure and evidently had no economic pressure urging him to write *comedias* as did so many of the other early dramatists. Contrary to what has been said, there is no documentary evidence of his having received the Licentiate nor of his having taken Holy Orders.[19] We do have documents that show he remarried in 1612 after the death of his first wife and little more than two years before his own demise.

Besides the pseudobiblical play, *La vida y muerte de Judas*, [The Life and Death of Judas],[20] he has left us four, perhaps five, historical plays, two of which (his best known works) deal with his wife's illustrious ancestor: *La próspera* and *La adversa fortuna de Ruy López de Avalos* [The Prosperous and The Adverse Fortune of Ruy López de Avalos].[21] The others are *La privanza y caída de don Alvaro de Luna* [The Rise and Fall of Don Alvaro de Luna],[22] *El premio de las letras por el Rey Felipe II* [The Reward of Letters by King Philip II],[23] and the questionably attributed play *El rey perseguido y corona pretendida* [The Persecuted King and Desired Throne],[24] which until the present century existed only in an unpublished manuscript of the National Library in Madrid. That work is assigned, by the scribe, to a Licenciado Poyo of Salamanca who may or may not be Salucio del Poyo. Although the play was almost certainly written during the period in which Salucio was writing for the Spanish stage and shows some of the principal characteristics for which he is known, it is not certain that he was in Salamanca or that he received the Licenciate. Given the questionable nature of such scribal attributions, proof of a more substantial kind must be presented either to support or to deny his authorship. Salucio's importance, recognizing the evident weaknesses of the works we have, lies in his influence on later poets who chose to rework his materials into superior dramas or to make use of elements from them with which to better their own.

Five of Salucio's six plays are based on historical matter and one is a novelistic work about the biblical traitor Judas. All six suffer from a surfeit of characters and incidents. Others, if not Salucio del Poyo, were quite aware of the fact. On the manuscript of *The Persecuted King,* which with sixteen named characters and various supernumeraries requires the smallest cast of any of the plays, the copyist added a note to the effect that the work would be performed, by doubling the parts, with no more than fifteen actors. Salucio's other plays have as many as thirty-two named characters.

A second weakness in Salucio's theater is the inability to handle dramatic structure, avoiding the linear, episodic manner so typical of early history plays. Even the novelistic *Life and Death of Judas* fails as drama for this reason. Not one of the five historical plays has the visual or auditory action so necessary for the appeal of pageantry if it is to overcome the lack of shape and definition inherent to its underlying structure.

Some of the structural instability results from Salucio's avoidance of love intrigues as dramatic material. First to note this missing element in his theater was Mesonero Romanos, but he followed the lead no further.[25] A study of all five plays shows that the few women characters who are present are, indeed, mere accessories to the plays. Unlike the majority of his contemporaries, Salucio does not end his plays with the conventional marriages. The women of his works exist as necessary but unimportant appendages to the actions of the male characters. Only one female character takes on any importance even momentarily. In *The Persecuted King* Violante, the wife of Alphonse the Wise (*Alfonso el sabio),* disguises herself as a male student in order to follow him to the

University of Palencia (predecessor of Salamanca), where the scholar king is visiting. Underscoring the picture of him as a "persecuted" king (the opening scene presents him as the butt of a student hazing reminiscent of those described, quite scatologically, in at least two picaresque novels of the time), Violante tells her husband the story of the small tasty fish so in love with goats that those who want to capture them dress in a goat's skin. When the fish jumps out of the water to kiss its beloved goat, it can be caught. Just so, she says, she has disguised herself as a student, hoping to end the neglect in which she has found herself. Because she is at last pregnant (one is tempted here to question the intended application of the imagery native to the tale she tells), Alphonse accepts Violante and refuses a proposed marriage to Christine, Princess of Norway. Christine is, instead, married to his brother Fernando, who promises to get Christine the throne she had come to Spain for, even if he must fight his brother to obtain it. This important conflict, well developed in the first act, is left at this point and never resolved. The rest of the play focuses instead on the rebellion of Alphonse's rash son Sancho the Fierce *(Sancho el bravo)*.

If, as Lope de Vega said in his dedication to *Los muertos vivos* [The Living Dead],[26] Salucio was the first to recognize the dramatic contrast found in the theme of the rise and fall of Ruy López de Avalos, those plays were not his first attempt to stage the theme of fickle Fortune. He had treated it earlier in *The Rise and Fall of Don Alvaro de Luna* where he attempted to study both aspects in one three-act play.

Act I. Don Alvaro is presented as a courtier and the baptism of his son is honored by the presence of King Juan II. Don Alvaro is the subject of much envious gossip as others witness the favors he receives (often as the result of some rather open hints to the King) from King Juan who backs him against all opponents, particularly the treacherous Princes of Aragón. A madman, claiming to have been apprentice to an astrologer, enters to prophesy and warns Alvaro of difficulties to come. When King Juan is attacked by the troops of the Aragonese, he faces them alone, ordering Alvaro to save himself. The peace settlement requires the banishment of Alvaro from the kingdom for a period of six years. The King agrees to this, but after his own position is once again assured, he banishes the Princes and commutes the sentence of his friend Alvaro.

Act II. Shortly after the death of the Queen, Alvaro returns from exile bringing with him a concluded agreement for the marriage of the King to the Portuguese Princess. King Juan, unaware of Don Alvaro's plans, has proposed marriage to a French Princess. At first angry at Alvaro's boldness in substituting brides, a substitution symbolized by the surreptitious exchange of portraits, the King gives in to the wishes of his favorite when Alvaro points out the need for the support of Portuguese troops. Later, Don Alvaro is presented as countermanding the King's direct orders in a battle against the Princes of Aragón. Several times, Alvaro is shown caring for his own interests above all. For example, on his own initiative he frees the Princes who have been captured by the royal forces, demanding their gratitude in exchange for this favor. Don Alvaro's pride is even more evident when, in the presence of the King, he draws his sword and kills a disobedient soldier. Still, King Juan does not punish him. Instead Alvaro receives even more, and greater, honors.

Act III. The new Queen and other enemies obtain a *carte blanche* with which they hope to effect the arrest of Don Alvaro. Before they can do so, Alvaro murders the treacherous secretary Vivero, and King Juan at last orders his arrest. The Queen convinces her husband of the need for an open trial. Sentence is passed by the judges and the death warrant is prepared. The King, after much wavering, is forced to sign the warrant. Alvaro is beheaded, and his page Moralicos is left to beg alms with which to bury the body.

Salucio's *comedia* presents Don Alvaro as a human being flawed by pride, stubbornness, and avarice, but with qualities of intelligence, generosity, and daring that endear him to the King. The play suffers from the fact that the action, which at its base has all the conditions needed for real tragedy, is presented through a series of unconnected episodes that seem to lead in too many directions at the same time. There is no lack of conflict in this case, rather there are too many conflicts with a consequent lack of climactic contrast. Essentially the work fails as tragedy because the audience feels, when all is said and done, that Don Alvaro got what he richly deserved.

Salucio does make at least one noteworthy use of strophic variety. To present the King's lament over the need to sentence his friend, he composed a passage of *quintillas* in which Salucio not only uses the consonantal rhyme scheme typical of the strophe, but he does so in such a way that throughout the entire passage alternate consonantal rhyme-sets rhyme in assonance *(i-e)* as well. The *quintillas* are at the same time a *romance,* a true poetic *tour-de-force!* The effect of the repeated high front vowel sounds in rhyme position is strikingly plaintive.

Antonio Mira de Amescua, in his treatment of the same plot material in *La adversa fortuna de don Alvaro de Luna* [The Adverse Fortune of Don Alvaro de Luna],[27] eliminates most of the extraneous matter, sharpens the contrasts, and adds psychological depth to the characters, shaping the story into one of the few pure tragedies of the Spanish Golden Age theater. Mira's play, too, begins with a baptism *(in),* the baptism of the King's son at which Alvaro is honored by being named godfather, Admiral, Constable, and Comendador. This is an opportunity to show the favorite at the peak of his fortune. The same *loco* astrologer appears, but in the person of the *gracioso* ("fool") Linterna who, rather than appear in only this one scene, is present throughout the work as a source of current political and literary satire, the only comic relief in the entire work. The identical pun that Salucio used appears among the prognostications. When Alvaro is warned to avoid the *cadalso* (executioner's block) he chooses to interpret the word as *Cadahalso* (a small town in Castile) a place that he can easily avoid. In Mira's play the exchange of portraits and Alvaro's insistence on the Portuguese marriage is made the pivotal point in the work *(pp),* the place in the dramatic action at which the protagonist's trajectory becomes fixed in its final tragic descent.[28] Mira presents Don Alvaro as a real hero, whose only flaw is the quite human desire for the gratitude of others. He is in conflict only with the inexorable turn of Fortune's wheel. The Queen who owes her position to Alvaro, moving the King's hand as he signs the death warrant, actually performs this action. In Mira's play, the lament of King Juan is made all the more effective because, rather than occurring before sentence is passed and approved, it occurs after the execution has taken place when the King realizes too late that Alvaro was really innocent of the charges made against him *(ec).* Mira de Amescua, writing in 1621–1624, was able to rearrange the materials used by Salucio del Poyo and mold them to basic dramatic structure, immeasurably strengthening the play by doing so.

The two plays on the fortune and misfortune of Ruy López de Avalos (precedent in history if not in composition to that of Don Alvaro) that Salucio uses to treat the theme of Fortune are, at least thematically, unified as the earlier play is not. Both works, however, are overladen with characters, plots, and incidents.

The Prosperous Fortune (a play with twenty-one named characters) shows the favorite's rise from slave of the Moors to the highest position in the kingdom of Castile in spite of multiple plots by Moors, English, and Portuguese to bring him down. The only element apparent in Ruy López's character to explain this rise is his remarkable daring, and the play at times falls to the level of pageantry (without the necessary appurtenances) as successive battles and royal audiences are presented on stage. Still there are scenes of interest that later authors chose from the play to decorate their own. An example is the scene in which the Princess's portrait falls from the wall, blocking the door to the King's chamber, thus saving him from the poison being brought to him by a Jewish doctor. This scene was used later by Tirso de Molina in his *La prudencia en la mujer* [A Woman's Wisdom].[29]

The Adverse Fortune, with thirty-one named characters, treats the fall of Ruy López, and like the Don Alvaro play was reworked by Mira de Amescua into a more successful version, one in which Mira eliminated the odd and distracting elements and made the work serve more clearly as a dramatic antecedent as well as a historical one to the Don Alvaro play. Again, Mira's use of Salucio's work is undeniable. Using the dramatic materials supplied to some extent by Salucio, he followed the same procedure as in the Don Alvaro work developing the theme into a well-structured drama.

The Reward of Letters tells the story of the rise of a peasant lad named Juan Martín Pedernal, changing his name in the course of the play to the more *culto* form Siliceo. He eventually becomes Archbishop of Toledo, Primate of Spain, under the rule of Philip II. Juan Martín teaches himself to read and write, goes to the University as servant to a wealthy young man, wins the chair of Professor in the Oppositions (Oral examinations) against all others including his own former master, is chosen to become the tutor of Prince Philip, and when Philip succeeds to the throne after the abdication of his father Charles V, is named Archbishop. The play lacks interest except for some prurient passages contrasting the lives of his servants with that of the cleric.

Salucio's *Life and Death of Judas* is an interesting pastiche of legendary tales and Biblical characters. In a fashion similar to Tirso's *El condenado por desconfiado* [Condemned for Lack of Faith], with which it enjoys other similarities as well,[30] the play presents two characters in contrary motion. Judas starts out as a bad character and gets steadily worse until the demons drag his body offstage. Dimas, the Good Thief, is presented as never really having stolen anything or committed any crime. He is forgiven his human sins by Christ as he dies on the cross and is taken with Him into heaven. The work, however, suffers from a lack of dramatic suspense. One knows the outcome beforehand, and therefore it degenerates into a catalog of opposite good and bad actions and contrasting qualities of the two protagonists. This play, too, has far too many characters, an oversupply of incidents, and a lack of dramatic structure.

Andrés de Claramonte y Corroy

By the year 1603, Claramonte was known as a playwright and producer since he is cited—as are most of the early writers of *comedias*—by Rojas Villandrando.[31] Still, we have no definite evidence pointing to any one of his works that may date from this very early period. A native of Murcia, documents show his presence as a director-producer of plays in Madrid in the years 1614 and 1615, in Seville from 1617–1623, and again in Madrid in 1623. He died there in 1626. We have the texts of about fifteen plays that can be attributed to him with some degree of certainty. In addition, he has frequently been cited as a possible author of *La estrella de Sevilla* [Sevillian Star], one of the finest plays of the Golden Age.[32] It has been suggested as well that he may have had an important hand in reworking that most important of all *comedias, El burlador de Sevilla* [The Trickster of Seville], into its present state.[33] It is not clear how much of these works, if any, is due him either as author or as a producer-director who worked with the originals of others, adding to them or changing them as suited either his artistic or business purposes. His works as a whole exhibit a remarkable ability to stage plays (he was, after all, primarily a manager of a stage company) in such a way as to increase their popular appeal. In many instances, the plays seem to be built from bits and pieces lifted from the works of others; they give the appearance of a montage aimed at pleasing a less than critical or intellectual audience. Besides their nature as composite works, his *comedias* show a general tendency to concern themselves with action and spectacle. They abound with scenes requiring more or less elaborate stage machinery in order to present the miraculous and supernatural events upon which they center. Also typical of Claramonte's theater is the way in which he presents the typed characters, incidents, and plots from which his plays are constructed, and leads them to an unusual (if somewhat unprepared for) denouement.

Sturgis Leavitt, the critic who first studied Claramonte's work in any depth, found that the plays are remarkably deficient in humor, even— Leavitt complains—when the *gracioso* descends to the vulgarity that in that time was so often the source of laughter.[34] Nevertheless, a careful study of the staging required for the works refutes that conclusion to some extent and we find that, indeed, a generous helping of visual humor is easily found in the actions called for in performance. What is obviously missing, as noted by Leavitt, is the wit and verbal humor found in so many *comedias* of other authors. This aspect of Claramonte's style underscores what has already been identified as his primary interest in stagecraft.

El valiente negro en Flandes [The Brave Black in Flanders].[35] Among Claramonte's better works, this *comedia* merits attention if only because of its unusual theme. *The Brave Black* is just one of several plays by Claramonte with a black principal. This fact surely indicates the presence of at least one black actor of sufficient status to be given lead parts—probably in Claramonte's Sevillian company— during the second decade of the seventeenth century. The play is, in spite of its overly large cast and tendency towards an episodic structure, rather well put together and in this aspect is at least one step forward from preceding historical pageant-plays.

Act I. The work begins with a series of expository scenes presenting the proud and rather violent nature of the *negro* Juan, son of the slave Catalina. In fact the opening scene is designed to capture the attention of the audience and get the action off to a moving start as Juan erupts onto the scene seemingly fighting off a whole platoon of the Spanish army and insisting on his "honor" *(in)*. The body of the play itself, however, clearly develops from Leonor's intercession with the Captain to save the life of Juan. This brings her face to face with the Captain, Don Agustín *(ra)*. This worthy, it seems, has been avoiding the confrontation since he has no desire to carry out a promised marriage to her that had been arranged earlier by Leonor's father, who is now dead *(ex)*. Struck by her beauty, when he finally sees her, Don Agustín offers his hand and she accepts on the condition that he stay in Mérida rather than go off to the war in Flanders *(ra)*. On the basis of this promise he enjoys the lady's favors before making their marriage public *(ra)*. Agustín breaks his word and leaves for Flanders as well, but he is followed by Leonor (disguised as a soldier) as she seeks to maintain her honor *(ra)*. In Flanders, Juan proves himself a hero as he single-handedly captures a band of Germans *(ra)*. He is rewarded by the Duke of Alba who, in addition to promoting him to sergeant, renames him somewhat ironically *(Alba* being Latin for "white") Juan de Alba *(ra)*. Claramonte's use of prurient material to no dramatic purpose—other than to keep the interest of his audience—is apparent in the final scene of this act. Leonor, dressed as a page, arrives at the Duke's camp and offers to sleep with Juan. Juan, sure that the rather effeminate appearing page "Esteban" is looking for a homosexual bedpartner, refuses, overreacting in such a horrified manner as to make the situation truly comic for his seventeenth-century audience.

Act II. Juan, promoted to sergeant, incurs the enmity of the former sergeant, adding that problem to the dislike of Don Agustín as a difficulty he must face *(ra)*. There is much sexual humor scattered throughout these scenes as, for example, when "Esteban" tells Juan "he" has found a soul-mate in the person of Agustín. At the mid-point of the play, after further heroics on his part, Juan is promoted to captain and is, perforce, accepted on equal footing by all *(pp)*. Juan witnesses an ardent embrace between "Esteban" and Agustín and his suspicions about the latter's sexual interests are confirmed *(rt)*. Agustín receives a letter from home advising him that a marriage has been arranged for him with Doña Juana. He agrees since, after all, Leonor cannot now make a fuss without publicly advertising her own lack of discretion and lost honor *(pt)*. Juan captures the Prince of Orange himself, and is rewarded for this deed by being sent to the royal court at Madrid *(rt)*. Leonor at last identifies herself to Juan and asks his help in forcing the recognition of her marriage to Agustín *(rt)*.

Act III. Juan arrives at court to be named a Grandee of Spain just in time to be present at the projected wedding of Agustín and Doña Juana *(rt)*. Through a series of well-worked-out strategies that at times misdirect the audience as to their real purposes *(pt)*, Juan manages so that Don Agustín publicly acknowledges Leonor as his wife *(ec)* and Claramonte's work ends with the promise of a sequel to this rather unusual play.

The *comedia* certainly starts well with an exciting opening scene, and most of the principal elements in it seem to develop from the initiating incident as is to be expected; however, there are far too many unconnected episodes and minor characters for the play to have any real strength. There is a lack of essential connection between the main plot (the rise of the negro Juan to a position of honor and respect) and the secondary plot (the struggles of Leonor to force Agustín to carry out his marriage promise). In fact, one is never really sure whether the play centers about one or the other and, except that Claramonte ends the piece with the promise of a sequel, there are few clues as to which is the main center of interest. The play is, nevertheless, typical of Claramonte's writing from a structural point of view. It is characteristic in stylistic terms as well, since the language is replete with the Gongoristic clichés and flights of verbal fancy for which his writing is known.

By far the best known of Claramonte's authentic works, and certainly most interesting for the literary connections it exhibits, is *Deste agua no beberé* [I Won't Drink This Water].[36] This play is a different version of the same legend dealing with Doña Mencía de Acuña and Don Gutierre Alfonso Solís that is the basis for the plot of Calderón's sensational honor drama *El médico de su honra* [The Physician to His Own Honor].[37] Another item of interest of the same vein in the work is the appearance (with echoes of *The Trickster of Seville*) of a servant girl, Tisbea, in scenes replete with *water-sex* imagery and the centering of the play around two false accusations: one made by the King Don Pedro against Mencía, and the other made by Doña Juana Tenorio (!) against Gutierre.

Act I. The play begins with two episodes that call for some finesse in staging but lead nowhere in terms of drama. King Pedro the Cruel, hurrying to Seville, is halted first by a farmer who prophesies his future in the internecine war he is carrying on with his brother. The farmer magically disappears when the soldiers accompanying the King try to arrest him. He leaves behind a shroud. Then a country girl appears to continue the prophecy and she disappears leaving behind a bloody dagger *(ex?)*. The King, tired and worn, seeks to rest outside the castle of Don Gutierre Alfonso, now absent, and sends to ask that food and drink be brought to him. Doña Mencía, wife of Gutierre, and Tisbea come to serve him personally *(in)*. Claramonte uses this as an opportunity to build a sensuous atmosphere through the imagery involved as both food and water are offered to the King. Mencía invites the King to spend the night in the castle and, sure that she is welcoming him not only to her board but to her bed as well, he gladly accepts *(ra)*. Talking to her brother Diego at the court, Doña Juana Tenorio falsely accuses Gutierre of having seduced her under promise of marriage and then having married Mencía instead *(ex)*. In spite of Mencía's precautions, the King enters her bedroom and when she rebuffs him, he offers (like the biblical King David) to see that her husband dies leaving her free to marry him and the throne *(ra)*. She screams for help. As others come, she saves both her own honor and that of the King by declaring that he had arrived before they had come with the needed aid *(ra)*. Still, this does not save her from the anger of the scorned monarch. When Diego Tenorio appears before the King to plead for justice for his sister Juana, King Pedro sees a chance for revenge *(ra)*. Gutierre returns to report his victory in battle and, rather than the reward he expected, the King gives him a letter in which he orders Mencía's death *(ra)*.

Act II. Because he cannot bring himself to carry out his orders, Gutierre finally confesses to Mencía that her execution has been ordered. She tells him how it came about *(ra)*. Diego Tenorio arrives, finds that Gutierre has not executed his wife and sends her out with Don Gil, giving him the orders for her death *(pp)*. Diego then demands that Gutierre carry out his promise of marriage to Juana *(pt)*. Gutierre claims that the accusation against him is false and he is taken to court under arrest so the King can administer justice *(rt)*. Gil befriends Mencía and, instead of killing her, frees her. She disguises herself as a shepherd.

Act III. When Diego comes to the court with Gutierre, the latter still maintains his innocence and is granted a request for trial by battle *(pt)*, a trial in which he "proves" his claim *(rt)*. The action of the plot is interrupted by an episode that seems to steer the play in a new direction: believing his beloved Mencía to be dead, Gutierre wanders off and, in a remarkable scene, he sees her reflected in a woodland pool; however, neither realizes the actual presence of the other *(pt)*. In the meantime, the King is bringing matters to a head. He threatens Juana with life in a convent *(rt)* and orders that both Gil and Gutierre be executed for failure to obey direct orders *(ec)*. The frightened and repentant Juana admits her falsity and King Pedro then demonstrates his "just" rather than "cruel" nature by bringing the still alive Gutierre, Mencía, and Gil together, blessing the marriage of Mencía and Gutierre, and arranging a suitable marriage for Juana as well *(dt)*.

Obviously neither *The Brave Black* nor *I Won't Drink* is up to the standard—poetic or structural—set by the writers of the Golden Age. What they do offer lies in the realm of audience appeal: action, inventive use of stage machinery, and topical interest *(i.e.,* the supernatural, sex, and violence). Indeed, Claramonte seems to be at his best in dealing with spectacle. In at least four of his other plays he stages pagan religious rites, a surefire trick for the lover of visual effects (as any Hollywood director knows), and especially so in seventeenth-century Spain. In the *El mayor rey de reyes* [Greatest King of Kings],[38] another of Claramonte's plays requiring a black in a leading role, he presents the Magi, their lives before and after their trip to Bethlehem and the battles they face as they attempt religious changes on their return to their respective homes. This plot allows for repeated presentations of various rites to honor the Sun God, several supernatural apparitions, miraculous occurrences, and a staged hand-to-hand battle between two women.

In *La ciudad sin Dios* [The Godless City],[39] the story of Jonah not only requires that he be vomited onto the stage from the mouth of a large *(papier-mâché)* fish nicely described in the stage directions, but the wickedness of Nineveh calls for pagan worship and a wild palace orgy. Claramonte uses this opportunity to give the play a prurient side. In one scene, the insatiable King of Nineveh, tired of standard orgiastic activities, asks if there is nothing new in the way of sexual practice that might interest him. His wicked counsellor Delio suggests that he might make love to his own mother. This shocking advice is refused only because the lady concerned is too aged to interest the King. Delio then suggests a sister as a good possibility. That advice is eagerly accepted.

El nuevo rey Galinato [The New King Gallinato],[40] picks up the popular theme of the Chilean Indians who fought off the conquering

Spanish for so long. This work calls for the sacrifice of an Indian Princess to the Sun God. The play, *Púsome el sol, salióme la luna* [My Sun Has Set, My Moon Has Risen],[41] that deals with Saint Theodora is another case in point. Among other things, the Saint takes off her clothes (on stage)[42] as a symbol of her acceptance of Christ, walks on water to save her enemy Lesbia from a man-eating crocodile, and adopts the habit of a monk in order to take part in the religious life of a monastery. The play gives ample opportunity for pagan worship to be staged, combining it with a sexual theme (Lesbia is a priestess of Venus), as well for miraculous conversions. The action in which Alcina, having given in to the sexual desires of Zurdo, tries to seduce the "monk" (Theodora) is typical of Claramonte's habit of piling incidents one upon another. When Alcina fails, she seeks revenge (for having been so scorned) by keeping the monk's cape for later use as proof of her accusation that "he" is the father of her child, a charge that Theodora easily refutes. Many of the varied wickednesses of the four plays described here (and those of several other works among Claramonte's production as well) are, of course, foiled by Christ and the Virgin Mary who appear quite regularly, as needed, on stage.

Although Claramonte's works as a whole seem to be lacking in intrinsic literary value, and in spite of the obviously bad taste (for any age) in which they were written, they are interesting as a compendium of the devices that could be and were used on the Spanish stage of the seventeenth century.

Other Dramatists and Conclusion

Finally, some minor playwrights of this period have not been studied here at all: the *Licenciado* Mexía de la Cerda, Juan Grajales, Julián de Armendáriz, Alonso Hurtado de Velarde, Gaspar de Avila, Alonso Remón, Lucas Justiniano, Juan de Ochoa, Diego de Vera, and Juan de Valdivieso, to name those for whom texts are extant and available. All of these are mentioned in Rojas Villandrando's work of 1602.[43] The omission is made in full knowledge of what they wrote but is necessary because of space limitations and because a review of their work would, in my opinion, add little to our understanding of the points on which this chapter is centered; however, others may still find much of value in their *comedias*.

As a group, the early *lopistas* show some tendencies in common: (1) they were attempting in one way or another to overcome the episodic nature of the early theater, even as they dealt with the historical materials so popular at the time, combining them with novelistic elements as they sought dramatic structure and unity as a means of strengthening their plays; (2) they were quite aware of the physical problems of staging and of the nature of the drama as an interaction of audience, player, and playwright. This awareness led them to write plays that would appeal to all. They made individual contributions to the development of the *comedia* as well.

Miguel Sánchez did, indeed, as Lope de Vega maintained, develop the technique of deceiving with the truth to a fine point but he failed, particularly in the third acts of his plays, to master the necessary structure and techniques for maintaining suspense. Salucio del Poyo, although he repeatedly fell into the trap of the episodic, did succeed in definitely tying the theme of Fortune to Spain's historical past. He did this so well that the best plays written on the theme in the years to follow (those of Antonio Mira de Amescua) are better understood as reworkings of Salucio's plays than as independent productions. Claramonte should be seen as an innovator in stage functions and as one who clearly defined the tastes of his audience, the common herd that flocked to the public theaters in his day. His works are more interesting for what they demonstrate in the way of actual staging than they are for literary reasons.

Chapter Three
Lope's Challengers (1621–1630)

The decade of 1621 to 1630 is an interesting one in the development of the *comedia* because during these years vital changes occurred in the mixture of materials from which the genre was developing. These were not changes in style alone, although the differing poetic modes are apparent in the works, nor did the poets master problems of dramatic structure as well as the playwrights of the following decade were to do. As we have seen, the important political and economic alterations of the period brought with them concurrent transmutations in the theater, as the audience to which the drama was directed changed. We should try to comprehend the differences in these two areas before taking up the actual stylistic and structural permutations in the works of the minor dramatists since, to some extent, new political, economic, and social factors explain developments in the more purely literary areas.

Hugo Rennert summarized the situation quite accurately in his *The Spanish Stage in the Time of Lope de Vega.*[1]

Of the kings of Spain during the period with which we are concerned, Philip the Second [d. 1598] seems to have lent no support to the theater nor to have favored it in any material way. Indeed, nothing could have been more opposed to his gloomy religious character, and while Philip the Third [d. 1621] inherited much of the sombreness of his father's nature, which toward the close of his life developed into a like religious fanaticism, he seems not to have been averse to the stage and even had a theater built in the palace for private representations, though this was probably due more to the interest and delight which the Queen took in such performances. . . . With the succession to the throne of Philip the Fourth in 1621, at the age of sixteen. . . , a more favorable period for the drama was inaugurated. He was a generous patron of art and literature and was especially an ardent admirer of the theater. . . . With Philip the Fourth the theater was a ruling passion in which perhaps his inordinate weakness for the *comediantas* played no less a part than his admiration for the *comedia.*

N. D. Shergold, too, notes the changes that occurred with the increase of royal patronage under Philip IV.[2] This is best deduced from his description of functions in the royal theaters at Aranjuez and at the *Alcázar* (Royal Palace) in Madrid. These two theaters were the true center of the Spanish stage during the decade of the 1620s and only surrendered their primacy upon the opening of the Buen Retiro's theater in the early 1630s. The royal backing was reflected in the accompanying development of movement toward private performances as various nobles—including those in the provinces—tried to match regal tastes and habits.[3] The fact that these court theaters existed alongside the public *corrales* resulted in an interesting interreaction as each influenced works presented in the other. Successful plays from the public stage would be prepared for performance at the royal (and other private) theaters quite as regularly as the reverse would occur. Naturally, the differing audiences and staging conditions resulted in more or less extensive changes (the work of the poets themselves, the producer-directors of the acting companies, or the actors who performed the pieces) to accommodate the plays to staging possibilities, actors' abilities, or audience sensitivities.

The dramatists' manner of writing was affected not only by the theater and the specific audience to which their works were aimed but, especially in this decade, authors began to see possibilities for further income from their work in the field of publication. Consequently, we find an increasing awareness on the part of the poets of the literary aspects of their works. The spadework performed by Lope de Vega and the enterprising printers who published his works and that of other dramatists—with or without their permission or knowledge—was to bear golden fruit in the decade of the 1620s and thereafter as the *comedia* achieved a reading as well as a listening audience and authors retained or regained possession of their plays, gathered them into volumes, and sold them to printers.

An additional set of facts must be understood as we attempt to comprehend the literary climate in which the playwrights of the period worked. This ten-year period saw a decrease, not only absolute but relative, in the dramatic productivity of Lope de Vega. The vacuum left by that decrease in activity concurrent with an absolute increase in demand, was filled by the growing production of his contemporaries.

Using the dates arrived at by Morley and Bruerton, we find that we have nearly 120 authentic Lopean texts from the period 1601–1610, we have more than 100 from 1611–1620, yet we can identify barely fifty from the period 1621–1630 (and only a bare twenty from the last five years of Lope's life). It is precisely during this decade that we find the culmination of the theatrical work of Tirso de Molina, Juan Ruiz de Alarcón, and Antonio Mira de Amescua. The same period witnesses as well the beginning of the dramatic writings of Pedro Calderón de la Barca, Francisco de Rojas Zorrilla, Juan Pérez de Montalbán, and Agustín de Moreto.[4] Over and above the data showing a decrease in Lope's actual composition of plays, information available about performances given them reinforces this theoretical decrease in Lopean dramatic efforts during the decade. Palace records, for example, show that of forty-five plays performed before the Queen between October 1622 and February 1623, only five can be even tentatively identified as having been written by Lope de Vega. Not one of these five can be ascribed to him with any certainty, yet the other works for which authors are known represent a major cross-section of the dramatists working at the time: Tirso de Molina, Juan Ruiz de Alarcón, Antonio Mira de Amescua, Guillén de Castro, Juan Bautista Villegas, Antonio Hurtado de Mendoza, and Diego Jiméniz de Enciso.

If the story of the seventeenth-century *comedia* is one in which we can properly speak of two great cycles of playwrights: *Lopistas* and *Calderonistas*, a dichotomy for which there seems to be a critical as well as a historical basis, the decade of the twenties is best identified as one of transition. Often there have been attempts to identify Tirso de Molina, Juan Ruiz de Alarcón, or Antonio Mira de Amescua, all of whom wrote a major portion of their plays during these years, as key transitional figures. Yet Lope, too, made radical changes in his materials, style, and procedures during this same time period. The dramatic and poetic work of his earlier plays, like *Peribáñez* and *Los melindres de Belisa* [Belisa's Fastidiousness], are in sharp contrast to his *Punishment without Vengeance* and *Las bizarrías de Belisa* [Belisa's Generosity], plays written in the last five years of his life (1630–1635) in the period of Calderonian hegemony. These changes are found not only in Lope's plays but in those of Tirso, Mira, Alarcón, and the minor figures treated in this study in the form of: (1) a refinement of style and poetic language and, to some extent, the acceptance of a more cultured, Gongoristic style; (2) a tendency to include some sharp contemporary political and literary satire in the plays as a source of humor in contrast wih the earlier use of such characters as the country bumpkin, *morisco,* palace lackey, etc., for this same purpose; (3) an increasing seriousness of purpose in the drama, placing more importance than previously on its capacity for instructing as it entertained its audience; (4) a growing mastery of the methods and materials at the disposal of the poet in the form of a finer use of the principles of dramatic structure and poetic unity, and a recognition of the poetic forms (rhetorical as well as strophic) as an aid in expressing the emotional content of the plays. This increased mastery over the *comedia* is perhaps best seen in the relative simplification of plot structures as the dramatists learned to integrate plot and subplot into a unified whole.

What are the reasons for the decrease in Lope's dramatic production? Was it merely a matter of the aging poet being unable to keep up the frantic pace of his youth and middle age? Was it the result of royal disfavor? Or were the producers on a search for new names, materials, topics, and styles with which to titillate a satiated audience? Did the changes in style that distinguish the drama of the Lopean cycle from that of the Calderonian playwrights result from the demands of an increasing theatrically sophisticated audience? Or, did they come about because the poets who wrote for the theater were at last realizing the full power of the drama as a literary genre worthy of better treatment and more careful preparation, as has happened to the cinema during our century? What role did the increasing publication of *comedias* as material to be read play in these changes? Was the higher price that producers paid for new *comedias* an important factor in bringing new talents to the marketplace? Each of these questions suggests a likely answer and all probably acted or interacted to some extent to produce the situation of the twenties.

Even as Lope's production of *comedias* decreased, the number of plays and playwrights multiplied tremendously during the decade, making the choice of authors and plays about which to write a difficult one. In the previous chapter, the three (out of ten) poets who fit within our present limited goals could all be treated with some pretense of coverage, but here the choice is much more awkward both in terms of poets and plays. I have chosen to write at greater length about a few representative works written by three playwrights (Felipe Godínez, Diego Jiménez de Enciso, and Luis de Belmonte Bermúdez). I leave aside the works of at least twelve others, any one of whom is as worthy of study as those included. Again my choice is a personal one based on a reading of many *comedias* by all these "minor" dramatists. I feel that those chosen illustrate well the processes and work of this vital ten-year span.

Felipe Godínez (1585–1637)

Most of the little we know about the life of Felipe Godínez comes to us from the records of the Inquisition that deal with his trial before that body, a trial that was concluded in Seville on November 30, 1624, when he was thirty-nine years old.[5] Godínez was a priest, born in the town of Moguer about fifty miles from Seville, most probably in 1585, of a *converso* (converted Jewish) family. His grandfather had been tried earlier and condemned by the Inquisition and an uncle emigrated to northern Africa, where he openly reverted to Judaism.

The charges against Godínez stated that from his youth he had practiced Jewish customs, religious procedures, and dietary laws. Two of the plays he had written previously, *Las lágrimas de David* [David's Tears] and *Amán y Mardoqueo o a la horca con su dueño* [Haman and Mordecai or To The Gallows with His Master], were cited by the Inquisition as heretical in part since in them Godínez sets forth the proposition that the Angel Gabriel told Esther, that the Messiah was to be born of a mother who had been conceived without stain of original sin. Among the other charges were six elements lifted from sermons he had preached that were also claimed to be heretical: (1) Godínez interpreted scriptures to the effect that God had promised never to abandon the Hebrew people without having redeemed them; (2) he felt that this redemption had not yet taken place completely, that it was still in process; (3) he believed a knowledge of Hebrew to be necessary to a full comprehension of the scriptures and that, because of a lack of such knowledge, Saint Jerome had made errors in his translation, the *Vulgate;* (4) like the members of the *alumbrado* cult, Godínez conjectured that God had first created souls rather than bodies; (5) he did not believe in Christ's real presence in the Eucharist; and (6) he used a scandalous simile in explaining the mystery of the Trinity to his congregation. Comparing the Holy Trinity to an irrigation system, he said that God the Father related to the other persons as did the water wheel and other machinery to the whole, the Holy Spirit was likened to the flowing water, and Jesus corresponded to the donkey that served as its motive power.

Godínez, the only Golden Age dramatist to be condemned in person by the Inquisition, was found guilty and the punishment meted out was harsh. After being exposed to public shame, Godínez was imprisoned for one year, exiled from Seville for six years, and deprived of both the exercise and benefits of his clerical office. He seems to have gone to Madrid immediately upon his release since the autograph manuscript of his play *La traición contra su dueño* [Treason against His Master] is dated there in 1626. In 1630, he was at last reinstated to clerical office.

The earliest critical mention of Godínez as a writer of *comedias* is found in Cervantes's *Voyage to Parnassus* of 1614, in which he is cited as a newcomer to the field of dramatic writing. He is also cited by Pérez de Montalván and by Antonio Enríquez Gómez (the other Golden Age dramatist condemned by the Inquisition, but in his own absence). The fact that Godínez was not named by Lope in the *Laurel de Apolo* may well be due to the fact that Lope was writing that work while Godínez was under punishment by the Inquisition. Lope certainly did know him and his work since his signature, as official censor, is found on the manuscript of *Treason against His Master* approving the play for performance in 1626.

In his plays, Godínez seems to have been happier and had more success with the works that he wrote on Old Testament themes. A particularly fine play of this type is the *comedia Haman and Mordecai*. His works in the nature of popular secular drama are well developed and nicely worked out but seem to be forced and less free-flowing than the Old Testament plays. Among the better *comedias* in this group are *Treason against His Master* and *Aun de noche alumbra el sol* [Even by Night This Sun Gives Light]. The rest of Godínez's plays would be best classified as religious theater, since they are based on various Christian legends. These suffer from the extravagant, forced religiosity found in them that destroys all verisimilitude. Even so, one of these plays, *O el fraile ha de ser ladrón o el ladrón ha de ser fraile* [Either the Friar Must Turn Thief or the Thief Must Turn Friar], has merit and has previously been studied to some extent.[6]

Haman and Mordecai.[7] Among the several plays written by Godínez on Old Testament themes, *Haman and Mordecai or To the Gallows with His Master* is undoubtedly the best written and structured as a *comedia*. It is successful perhaps in part because the story, taken from the biblical book of Esther, was much less shopworn from overuse as a topic for a play than the more frequently used materials from Ruth or the history of King David from the book of Samuel; or perhaps because the substance from which this play was built was easier to handle dramatically than the story of Judith and Holophernes or the book of Job. All of these biblical accounts Godínez used as a basis for other *comedias*. Possibly the play seems to be better drama only because the plot is not as familiar as is the stuff from which the other plays are made and, consequently, the details that the dramatist must add and the liberties he must take with the original in order to achieve meaningful, artistic drama do not as apparently distort the base nor do they become so obtrusive as to destroy audience acceptance of the work.

Act I. King Ahasuerus has repudiated his former Queen Vashti *(ex)* and, to reward the advice given to him in the matter by Haman, orders that the latter be honored by all as if he were the King himself *(in)*. Hagai, a friend to Haman, suggests that a parade of beauties be brought before the King from which he may choose a new Queen *(ra)*. In a comically mirroring, pastoral interlude, a married couple Alfajad and Valda discuss the backgrounds of both Haman and Esther *(ex)*. Mordecai, Esther's uncle and guardian, comments on the proper Jewish attitude toward giving Haman the adoring reverence the King has ordered *(ex)*. While on a hunt with Haman, Ahasuerus sees Esther and falls in love with her *(ra)*. When Haman is refused the reverence due him by Mordecai, his wounded pride demands vengeance *(ra)* which he vows to take on all the Jewish people in the kingdom. Haman tells Ahasuerus the story of the troubles the Pharoah had with the Jews in Egypt and suggests that a pogrom would be in order *(ra)*. The King gives Haman his seal and permission to do what is necessary *(ra)*. Unaware that Esther is a Jewess, Ahasuerus chooses her from among the beauties paraded before him and orders Hagai to approach her with his proposal of marriage *(ra)*. There follows a remarkable scene (probably the source of some of the trouble Godínez faced at his trial) in which Esther is shown in a situation paralleling the Anunciation, making her an undoubted prefiguration of the Virgin Mary, and commenting on her róle as intercessor. Esther is warned not to reveal herself as Jewish and willingly goes off to join Ahasuerus *(ra)*.

Act II. Haman and his wife Zeresh seek the help of Teresh and Bigthan in a plot to assissinate Ahasuerus *(ra)*. As the latter pair discuss ways of accomplishing the deed, Mordecai overhears them and sends a warning to the King through Esther *(ra)*. Haman advises the King to insulate himself from importuning courtiers by ordering death for any who enter his presence without permission *(ra)*. Esther gets Mordecai's message of warning to Ahasuerus and the plotters are found *(ra)*. The King orders that Mordecai's service be entered in the official chronicles so as not to be forgotten *(pp)*. Esther's friendly approach to Zeresh is rebuffed *(pt)*. For a second time, Mordecai refuses to kneel to Haman and is forcefully thrown down by Haman's companions. Again pointing to the *Old Testament* as a prefiguration of the *New*, Mordecai reminds Haman of Daniel's prophecies *(rt)*. Haman denies the truth of these and tells Mordecai of his edict ordering the registration and confinement of all Jews in the kingdom *(pt)*. Mordecai, in an effort to get this news to the King through Esther, meets her at a window of the palace *(rt)*. She reminds him of the new law about entering the King's presence unbidden and points out that to do so means her own death *(pt)*. Haman, plotting to usurp the throne, is advised to build a gallows on which to hang Mordecai. He does so *(pt)*. Urged by Mordecai to take the risk, Esther enters the King's presence but is saved when Ahasuerus, before passing the death sentence advised by Haman, wants to know the identity of the culprit who has dared break his law *(rt)*.

Act III. Ahasuerus, in order to spend his time wisely, asks that the chronicle of his reign be read to him and is upset to find that Mordecai has not yet been rewarded for his earlier service *(rt)*. The King sends for Haman and seeks his advice about how best to reward a faithful vassal. Haman, in the belief that he is being asked to name his own reward, details a plan of public honor. Haman's pride is terribly wounded then, when he is forced to arrange the honors for Mordecai whom he would rather hang *(pt)*. This scene of jubilee is followed by several in which we see the courtiers changing sides (from backing Haman to supporting Esther) and scenes of comic relief. These are followed by the climactic scenes in which Esther, interceding for her people whose repentance has been symbolized by Mordecai and his sack cloth, pleads to Ahasuerus to undo the evil wrought by Haman *(ec)*. The King accedes to her wishes, placing Mordecai in charge of the changes, and orders Haman hung from his own gallows *(dt)*.

Haman and Mordecai is a *comedia* clearly based, in period and in content, on biblical sources with a minimum of novelistic material added. The additions are made principally for one of three purposes: for comic relief, to accentuate the motivation of the various characters, or to emphasize the author's didactic insistence, so typical of the Renaissance and Counter-Reformation, upon reading all pre-Christian materials as prefigurations of what was to come. This latter element is worthy of comment here because of the extraordinary lengths to which the poet has gone to achieve his purpose.

It is clear that in this play Godínez made every effort to impress upon his audience his reading of the book of *Esther* as an allegorical representation of Christian beliefs. In doing so, he tends to force the issue to the level of the objectionably obvious. Undoubtedly, it was this tendency to stretch the allegory in order to cover still unresolved dogmatic problems that got Godínez into trouble with the Inquisition, in spite of the fact that some of these were quite commonly believed. Too openly, the King is compared to the Creator, Haman takes on demonic proportions and attributes, Mordecai symbolizes the repentant sinner, and Esther is equated with the Virgin Mary (particularly in her role as mediatrix). For example, in the first act, seeing Esther for the first time, Haman compares her to the woman who has come to slay the *proud* dragon (himself). Hagai, when he approaches Esther with the King's offer of marriage, enters her presence respectfully and, according to the stage directions, "He kneels in the manner of the Angel greeting the Virgin." In his address to her he paraphrases the *Ave*, "Hail, Esther, full of grace. The Lord is with thee. Blessed art thou amongst women." As if this were not clear enough, Godínez has Mordecai explain to the audience in an aside that "Here we have represented a shadow, a figure of that time when a happy embassy came to the holy maiden through whom God was to take fleshly form." In the second act, when Esther appears before the King unbidden, he saves her life by touching her with his scepter (a phallic symbol?) saying, "The gallant who gave you his hand as you fell, is God himself." She responds with a paraphrase of the *Magnificat!* The point is even further underscored in the third act when Esther, too, tells the audience that she is a prefiguration of the mother of the Messiah who is yet to come.

Godínez's strophic practices in this play are normal for the period in which it was written. Indeed, except for the fact that in it we find some interesting and fairly early evidences of the influence of Luis de Góngora, the style of this play is not noteworthy. To illustrate this point one might cite the use of a Gongoristic expression in the play when the King hurries his messenger Hagai on his way with the expression *"Calzad alas diligente"* ("Shoe your diligent self with wings"). Again Mordecai, in his penance, states, *"Polvo soy, ceniza y nada"* ("Dust am I, ashes and nothing") in a paraphrastic echo of the final line from one of Góngora's immortal sonnets. Another interesting fact about the language of the play is that Godínez uses the same metaphor that was later to get him into trouble with the Inquisition when he employed it in a sermon: that of the irrigation system. Here, however, he applies the comparison to the working of the goddess Fortune rather than to the Trinity. There are, in addition, some wonderfully poetic moments in the work that distinguish it from others he wrote. One such is the beautiful monolog of the King, in the opening scene of Act III, in which he comments on the human condition and the miracle of motherhood.

Treason against His Master. [8] The interplay of the twin themes of faith and honor are the stuff from which this play, written shortly after the author's trial and condemnation by the Inquisition, is formed. [9] Godínez's contention is that Divine Providence will ensure eventual and proper punishment for all treason. In this case the treason is a willful and deceptive violation of the honor code through physical act and through false accusation.

Act I. Inés, having been violated by Sancho, appeals to her cousin, the Queen, for help in arranging a marriage with him *(ex).* Since the King has no direct heir, the throne will pass to his sister Leonor, who is in love with Fernando, Inés's brother *(ex).* The king suggests that Leonor marry Sancho, but the Queen, hoping to arrange matters for

Inés, indicates her preference for a match with Fernando *(in)*. Leonor, who already suspects an incestuous relationship between Fernando and the Queen, grows even more suspicious and jealous when she overhears the Queen promise Fernando that he will one day be King *(ra)*. The Queen warns Sancho that he has evidently forgotten the one who loves him best and he, misunderstanding her intent, assumes that she is telling him of her own feelings for him *(ra)*. Sancho tries to enter the Queen's bedchamber one night while the King is away on a hunt and is driven out by the Queen with sword in hand *(ra)*. Realizing, finally, that what the Queen had said earlier dealt with Inés rather than herself, Sancho tells her that it was not she but Leonor whom he sought in the room. He adds that Leonor had earlier given herself to him and he had wanted to renew that relationship *(ra)*. Remembering Leonor's earlier statement that Sancho was her first love (a statement made in the hope of arousing Fernando's jealous response), the Queen is left disturbed as to how she might resolve the conflict of lost honor in both Inés and the Infanta Leonor *(ra)*. Inés tells her brother of Sancho's attempt on the Queen, of her own dishonor at his hands, and of his claim to have enjoyed Leonor's charms as well *(ra)*. Fernando faces Leonor and makes clear to her that Sancho cannot marry her because of his earlier commitment to Inés *(ra)*.

Act II. Sancho and his servant Guillermo plan to find out how far Fernando will go in insisting upon marriage in the case of Inés *(ra)*. In this process, Fernando's firm insistence on repayment for the debt of honor is made clear *(ra)*. Sancho then asks Leonor for her hand in marriage but she rejects him on the ground that he owes a debt elsewhere *(pp)*. This arouses Sancho to anger and he is loudly accusing all of plotting against him when the King enters *(rt)*. The King cautions Sancho to be more careful with his accusations. Sancho then tells the King, privately, that Fernando has been courting the Queen. His lie is corroborated by his aide Juan *(pt)*. In an attempt to test the Queen's honor, the King tells her that he has decided that Fernando should indeed marry Leonor *(rt)*. The Queen, thinking of the precedence that Leonor's honor as Infanta must take over that of Inés, urges the King to suspend that marriage. This plea confirms the King's suspicions of her guilt *(pt)*. Fernando now brings his complaint to the King: Sancho had violated Inés and should marry her *(rt)*. Leonor, learning that the Queen had effectively stopped a marriage to Fernando, is angered and hints to the King of an illicit relationship between Fernando and the Queen further confirming his doubts *(pt)*. The King orders Sancho to effect the arrest of Fernando and contemplates the imprisonment of the Queen *(pt)*. When Sancho faces Fernando, the latter challenges him to a duel *(rt)*.

Act III. While Fernando waits for Sancho at the appointed duelling place, a friend, Beltrán, comes to warn him of the King's suspicions. Beltrán, rather than leave as Fernando has asked, hides to see if he can be of service when Sancho does come *(rt)*. Rather than come to duel, Sancho enters with several companions and presents Fernando with the royal order for his arrest *(pt)*. The Queen is shocked to realize that the King's saddened mood is caused by his suspicions about her fidelity. She rebukes Leonor for her part in furthering his mistrust, insisting that she had only interfered with the marriage of Leonor to Fernando because of Sancho's claims of a previous intimacy with her *(rt)*. The King brings vials of poison intended for the Queen and Fernando but stops to listen to Leonor's insistence that the pair is blameless. He then appoints a judge to decide the matter *(rt)*. Sancho suggests that the judge torture Beltrán to find out the truth of things, planning to arrange it so that Beltrán will give information pointing to Fernando's guilt *(pt)*. The judge arrests Guillermo instead of Beltrán. The Queen tells the King of the incident in her bedroom with Sancho. Leonor, too, relates her story, insisting on the falsity of Sancho's accusation against her. Guillermo's testimony confirms their stories *(rt)*. Fernando is released. Sancho and Juan are ordered to drink the poison, but the Queen and Leonor intercede in their behalf *(ec)*. The situation is resolved when the King announces Fernando's marriage to Leonor and Sancho's with Inés who will follow her husband into exile *(dt)*.

Treason against His Master is a drama of the cape and sword variety built around invented stories dealing with the court of King Martin of Sicily and the eventual succession to the throne of Aragón by Fernando de Antequera as Fernando I. He was married to Leonor of Albuquerque and did indeed inherit the throne after the death of Martin in 1409; however, the novelistic materials upon which this *comedia* is based have no source in history or legend. The play seems to have been written more with an eye to delighting the audience with the stock *comedia* materials of honor and dramatic irony than with any didactic intent. A good reason for including the play here in spite of its evident weaknesses is that it is structured in the balanced, chiasmatic fashion that was to dominate the later *comedias.* However, the tension and suspense needed in a good dramatic piece is lacking in this, one of Godínez's better plays of secular theme.

In a section of the introduction to his doctoral dissertation that was omitted from the published version, Thomas C. Turner showed the symmetry basic to the structure of the play.[10] Among other tendencies, major elements of the plot as presented in the first act are reflected in reverse order in Act III: (1) the question of Inés's honor, (2) the problem of the succession to the throne, (3) Guillermo's questioning by the Queen, (4) the situation of the Queen's defense of her own honor when Sancho enters her bedroom, and (5) the false accusation made to the Queen about Leonor by Sancho. Each of these appears mirrored in the final act as: (5) Leonor convinces the Queen of Sancho's falseness, (4) the Queen tells the King of Sancho's violation of her chambers, (3) Guillermo confesses corroborating the truth of what the King has been told by Leonor and the Queen, (2) Fernando marries Leonor and will inherit the throne, and (1) Inés is married to Sancho, the thief of her honor. The very mechanistic quality of this ordering of materials may account in part for Godínez's inability to create suspense as the play approaches its denouement; yet the lack of tension is also due in part to the fact that he failed to create real characters in this play. One does not feel an emotional attraction to the stylized stock-figures of this work, a feeling that one does have about the convincingly created characters of the biblical play, *Haman and Mordecai.*

Unlike what happens in the even later play *Even by Night This Sun Gives Light,* there is very little use here of complex or extended metaphors or poetic images. The versification, even though it is correct and follows patterns usual to the *comedias* of the 1620s, seems somewhat cold and forced as if the author were writing stiffly under constraints strange and new to him. This seems true even though we know that in 1626, he had been writing plays since at least 1613.

The play *Even by Night*[11] shows Godínez's mastery of the forms and techniques of the *comedia* and is, perhaps deservedly so, the best known of his works. In it the parts go together well to make a unified artistic whole. The play deals with the efforts of Don Juan to ensure the legitimacy of his secret marriage to Doña Sol. Complications are provided by Costanza's love for him and Prince Charles's love for Costanza, a love that at times appears to be directed toward Sol, greatly to Juan's consternation. The dramatic climax of the play comes at the moment when Don Juan returns secretly from Castile and, meeting Sol in the garden, convinces her to allow him to spend the night with her even though she fears that he will be found with her, a fact that would mean his death. The poet uses several means to guarantee audience recognition of this key moment by underscoring the drama through action and language. The *gracioso* Neblí comments on Don Juan's conversation with Sol, using an interesting and unusual double pun, one sure to catch the attention of the audience.

> I, master to the cuckoo,
> a linnet's apprentice he:
> Don Juan was chanting on sol
> while I was singing on mi. (205b)

When Sol and Juan go offstage together, their actions are mimicked in humorous form by those of Neblí and the servant girl Inés who offers him food, drink, and warmth.

One other readily available play by Godínez has had previous critical comment: his *comedia* of Franciscan theme, *Either the Friar Must Turn Thief or the Thief Must Turn Friar*.[12] Two friends, Bruno and Luke, decide to go in opposite directions in their search for the road to success and happiness. Bruno enters the Franciscan order, not in answer to a religious call but in an attempt to find the secret of the friar's happiness. Luke seeks his gratification in a life without moral restraints. Bruno's false conversion becomes a sincere one through his contact with the founder saint, yet through it all he maintains his friendship with Luke, attempting to win him over to the religious life. Luke refuses and continues in his chosen life style of violence and wild women. Just as Luke is about to be captured and killed for his banditry, Bruno saves him by exchanging his habit for Luke's clothing and a promise to come when called. Bruno is killed as a result of the exchange of clothing and his soul is led to heaven by St. Francis whose death occurred simultaneously. Bruno calls Luke to join him, and because of his solemn promise, Luke does so by joining the order himself. The play is arranged in a chiasmatic, symmetrical structure of opposing contrapuntal trajectories much like that employed in the *El condenado por desconfiado* [Condemned for Lack of Faith] that has been questionably attributed to Tirso de Molina, or in Mira de Amescua's *There Is Neither Fortune Nor Misfortune until Death* and the Don Alvaro diptych. In *Either the Friar Must Turn Thief,* Godínez writes smoothly and well, successfully managing the florid poetic language with overtones of Góngora that infuses so much of his poetry.

Other religious plays by Felipe Godínez include his *San Mateo en Etiopía* [Saint Matthew in Ethiopia], *El soldado del cielo San Sebastián* [Heaven's Soldier, Saint Sebastian], *De buen moro buen cristiano* [From Good Moor to Good Christian], and *La virgen de Guadalupe* [The Virgin of Guadalupe].[13] Biblical plays by Godínez that are available to us include *Los trabajos de Job* [The Travails of Job], *La venganza de Tamar* [Tamar's Vengeance], and *Las lágrimas de David* [David's Tears].[14] Also available are four secular *comedias: Ludovico el piadoso* [Louis the Pious], *Basta intentarlo* [It's Enough to Try], *Acertar de tres la una* [Be Right About One Out of Three], *Los dos Carlos* [The Two Charlies], and *Celos son bien y aventura* [Jealousy Is a Fine Adventure].[15]

Diego Jiménez de Enciso (1585–1634)

From a relatively well-placed family, as is documented by key events in his life, the Sevillian poet Diego Jiménez de Enciso is best remembered for his historical plays. We know that he was born in Seville in 1585, spent a period of time (1618–1627) in Madrid, where he was supported by his friendship with the Count-Duke of Olivares, and passed the last few years of his life back in his native city having been made chief of staff (mayordomo) of the royal palaces there. He was named a member of the Holy Office (Inquisition) of Seville in 1612, and joined the confraternity of St. Ann in 1613, the same year in which he was also made a member of the ruling council of the city. In 1623, while in Madrid and after his mighty friend had assumed power as the King's favorite, he was admitted to the very distinguished Order of St. James (Caballeros de Santiago). He belonged, too, to one of the fashionable literary academies of Madrid, the Peregrina, while he was living there. At least one of his plays, *Júpiter vengado* [Jupiter Avenged], was written specifically for a palace production, with scenery and staging prepared by the great Italian designer Cosme Lotti.[16]

His worth and fame as a literary figure are attested to by the following citations: (1) he was mentioned as early as 1609 by Lope de Vega in his *Jerusalén conquistada* [Jerusalem Conquered], (2) Cervantes placed him among the worthy poets in his *Voyage to Parnassus* of 1614, (3) he was again praised by Lope in the *Laurel de Apolo,* and (4) Juan Pérez de Montalván included mention of him in *Para todos* [For Everybody] of 1632. Three of Jiménez de Enciso's *comedias* will be discussed here as examples of what he was able to accomplish in the genre: *Juan Latino, El príncipe don Carlos* [Prince Charles], and *Los Médicis de Florencia* [The Medicis of Florence].

Juan Latino. [17] The thesis of this quite unusual play is that learning is a function of native intelligence and personal desire, matters completely unrelated either to sex or to color. In order to achieve his didactic purpose, Jiménez de Enciso constructs the *comedia* around two themes, each of which has an historical base. One is built about the story of Fernando de Valor (descendant and heir apparent to the last of the Moorish kings of Granada), his leadership in and the eventual failure of the rebellion of the Alpujarra *moriscos* during the reign of Philip II. The other deals with the rise of a black man, Juan Latino, from slave to university professor. Romantic interest is provided as the latter overcomes all difficulties to gain the hand of Doña Ana (sister to the university's legendary founder) in marriage as well as his professor's chair. The two antithetical plots dealing, the one with the power of arms, the other with the value of letters, would each be sufficient in itself as the basis for a drama. In fact, the story of Fernando de Valor was used several times over by various Spanish Golden Age playwrights. In this play the theme of arms is placed in secondary position underscoring the prime thesis of the play since it is the story of a magnificent failure placed in contrapuntal opposition to a tale of success achieved through learning. If it were not for the fact that the work is so ordered that the one plot mirrors the other in carefully structured fashion and that the plots do have several points of contact, the play itself would suffer from a basic lack of unity. The materials, however, are very carefully handled as the author follows a plan of structural doubling that was successful also in the hands of Lope de Vega (i.e., *Fuenteovejuna*).

The mirroring effect of the two plot lines is seen throughout the play as episodes of one plot succeed episodes of the other. After the expository first scenes in which we find that the intellectual but none-too-pretty Ana, sister of Dr. Carlobal, is interested in finding a husband for herself but has rejected all suitors including Fernando de Valor (she rejects him on racial grounds), she follows the custom of St. John's Eve, saying her prayers and going to her balcony to ask the stars the name of him who is to be her husband *(in)*. She asks this just as, below her balcony, Juan Latino identifies himself to another as *"El negro Juanillo."* This episode of superstitions about the future is followed by one in which Fernando de Valor relates the astrological prognostication of his own future. The pivotal point in the play *(pp)* comes when one after the other Fernando and Ana come face to face with their problems. Fernando muses on a solution for the problem of whether or not to give in to the royal demands that all *moriscos* give up their weapons, clothing, customs, and language. He finally accepts leadership of the rebellion and the proferred crown at the same time that he reverts to Islam and rejects Christianity.

Ana, who is being tutored by Juan, finally realizes and accepts her love for him when, after a lesson in music, Ovid, and mathematics, he offers his love to her. The final climactic moments *(ec)* show the same doubling technique. Ana and Juan have had to resort to suing the court for approval of their marriage. Partly as a result of intervention by royal power, they are granted that relief, her brother accepts the inevitable, and Juan's former master reluctantly grants him his freedom. The celebration of these events is not dampened at all when the news of the final defeat of the Moors is brought in and the victorious Don Juan of Austria joins the group to honor the wedding and Juan Latino.

Points of even closer contact between plot and subplot further emphasize the essential structural unity of the play. Juan is slave to the very Duke who is expected to enforce the new laws promulgated against the Moors, peacefully if he can, by obtaining the cooperation of Fernando who is a member of his literary academy. At a meeting of that group attended by all, including Fernando, Ana, and Juan, the slave bests the other scholars in attendance by the force and lucidity of his arguments. The Duke, wishing to reward his slave, asks Dr. Carlobal to accept Juan as a student in his household much to the pleasure of both Juan and Ana (for intellectual reasons in both cases). When Don Juan of Austria comes to head up the royal forces in battle against the rebellious *morisco* population, he is so taken with Juan's intelligence and learning that he asks the Duke to emancipate the slave. Clearly throughout the work, both plot lines are closely related in theme as well as in action, and most certainly by the balanced antithetical nature of their themes (arms vs. letters) that so clearly reinforces the thesis of the play.

Of particular interest for what they tell us about the society and social views of the period are the passages in which (1) we are admitted as witnesses to the inner working of a Golden Age literary academy, (2) Juan Latino expresses his desire for freedom and equality, (3) Dr. Carlobal argues, in presenting Juan as a tutor to his sister, the lack of reason behind her color prejudice, (4) Ana insists on her rights as well as her desires for a complete education rather than the limited one that was often conceived of as proper for a lady in her position, (5) the author presents the formal "Oppositions" in which the various candidates for a vacant professorship, including Juan Latino, each attempt to win the approval of the university students.

Prince Charles. [18]   One of the first attempts to dramatize the tragic problem of Philip II and his son Charles, E. M. Wilson and Duncan Moir have stated of this *comedia* that "Many critics consider the play to be Enciso's masterpiece. It is a masterfully conceived drama, particularly strong in its contrasts of characterization, and a fine example of the application of the Aristotelian principle of the superiority of universal or poetic truth to historical truth."[19]

Act I. King Philip II receives birthday congratulations from the courtiers, all except his son Charles, who has refused to see his own father *(in)*. The Prince, whose mother had died at his birth, has been raised by others and feels rejected by his father who is always occupied with the business of state *(ex)*. When Charles is finally forced to come to his father (he wanted instead to go off to Alcalá), he falls into a raging fit *(ra)*. As soon as help arrives for the stricken Prince, the King leaves. At this Charles recovers and leaves for Alcalá to press his suit with Yolanda *(ra)*. He has sent Don Fadrique ahead to act as a go-between with his cousin, but Fadrique and Yolanda, unknown to the Prince, have been in love for some time past *(ra)*. The couple arrange a way to ensure Yolanda's safety if she cannot manage the Prince on her own *(ra)*. When, upon being rejected by Yolanda, Charles attempts rape, Fadrique explodes from his hiding place. The noise attracts the attention of his uncle, the Duke of Alba, who enters the room as well *(ra)*. The Duke saves the situation by distracting Charles with the announcement that he has arranged for the traditional ceremony in which the vassals pledge fealty to the Crown Prince *(ra)*.

Act II. Charles threatens the Duke of Alba in an attempt to get him to act as a go-between with his niece Yolanda *(ra)*. Later, he plots with the Flemish ambassador hoping to head up the new government the King is to appoint for that province *(ra)*. The contrasting characters of Charles and the King are clarified in successive scenes in which the Prince mistreats the Cardinal-President of the Advisory Council, and then the King deals with the Cardinal respectfully and properly as he attempts to solve the Flemish problem *(ra)*. The King and Prince are left alone to deal with their differences. The King tells Charles of the charges against him, but Charles, unrepentant and at the same time unaware that he has been spied upon, denies having any dealing with the Flemish *(pp)*. After Charles leaves, the King orders the assassination of the Ambassador *(rt)*. Charles, having bribed a servant girl to admit him to Yolanda's chambers in the palace, enters only to be faced again with an angry Fadrique. The Duke, too, enters but this time it is dark and he mistakenly engages Fadrique in battle while Yolanda, believing that she is helping her true lover, leads the Prince out to safety *(pt)*.

Act III. Yolanda faints when she discovers that she had aided Charles and is now his prisoner. When he goes to answer a call from his father, he has her locked in his room *(pt)*. The Ambassador is murdered in the adjacent chamber and Yolanda is rescued *(rt)*. The Prince returns and, intent upon rape, he attacks the Ambassador's body that has been substituted for that of the unconscious Yolanda. When he discovers his error and realizes that Yolanda has again escaped his grasp, he decides to leave at once for Flanders to lead the rebellion there *(pt)*. The Duke returns to tell the Prince that he, rather than Charles, has been named to rule in Flanders *(rt)*. King Philip calls for his son once more and tells him that he is about to abdicate and turn the responsibility of government over to him. He shows the Prince how much detail work there is to the job of ruling his far-flung kingdom *(pt)*. When Charles will not accept reason and refuses to repent of his insane actions, the King orders his imprisonment *(rt)*. Held prisoner in his chambers, the Prince falls ill with a fever and, dying, hallucinates a scene in which he sees his own ghost and the future of Spain down to the time of Philip IV's first marriage. Finally he repents his past actions and calls for his father in order to promise him that he will reform in the future, a future that no longer exists for him *(ec)*. The King states his belief that it was the nature of the Prince's mental illness that brought on his death, and then he commands the marriage of Fadrique to Yolanda *(dt)*.

The play is clearly based on historical materials from the recent past. It deals, in fact, with events of the years 1564–1568, a period just prior to the historical events used as the basis for the subplot of *Juan Latino* (1568–1571). In addition to the novelistic elements concerned with Yolanda, the play rearranges the material chronologically so as to compress the time element. Rather than carry the didactic tone of *Juan Latino, Prince Charles* studies the contrasting characters of the careful, phlegmatic ruler Philip II and that of his violent, sensual son. It is this tendency to study character and the poet's success in dealing with that aspect of the drama, an aspect often thought to be neglected in the Spanish *comedia,* that makes the play so well worth study. Especially is this so when the whole is presented in fine, carefully written verse and in such a well-structured dramatic format. The play is one of the finest of the decade, clearly having been written sometime shortly after 1623. It deals with a touchy subject but does so carefully in such a way as to bring forth the official explanation of the Prince's tragic death and to avoid any of the charges that were the subject of malicious court gossip.

The Medicis of Florence.[20]   This, perhaps the most famous of his plays in his own times, is, according to Wilson and Moir, "a superb and dignified tragedy on the treacherous and cowardly killing of Alessandro de Medici by his cousin Lorenzo."[21] The play is almost perfectly structured, with the minimum number of characters needed to present the story. Although he follows closely the plan of dramatic structure as set out here, the dramatist adds another and quite interesting device to his repertoire, one of particular interest because of the seventeenth-century habit of presenting an interlude between the acts of a performance. Such an interlude might detract from the audience's attention on the theme of the main play except that here Enciso ends both the first and the second acts with an unresolved climactic action, leaving the audience in suspense about what was about to happen.

Act I. A goodly portion of the first act is taken up with expository material, more than is usual in a *comedia,* probably because of the complicated nature of the plot to be presented. Yet the poet knew that the best way to attract the attention of his audience was to present an immediate conflict. That he does. Cefio Pazo comes on stage with drawn sword and in a raging fury. As his daughter tries to calm him, it becomes obvious that he is old and confused. This gives a chance for much of the background of the play to be presented in verisimile fashion. In spite of the fact that her father Cefio hates all the Medicis, Isabel is in love with Cosimo de Medici. Duke Alessandro (soon to marry Margaret the daughter of Charles V) and Lorenzo de Medici both want her as well. Alessandro's position as Duke of Florence has been assured by his marriage. Cosimo is his faithful but unappreciated aide. Lorenzo is a scoundrelly flatterer favored by the Duke *(ex).* A letter to Cosimo, written by Isabel, is delivered by her maid to Lorenzo instead *(in).* Cosimo comes to tell Isabel, not having seen the note, that Alessandro has found out about their love and has ordered him exiled. Since Alessandro has forbidden him to marry her, she is satisfied with his promise not to marry another without her permission *(ra).* As he leaves, Cosimo meets Lorenzo and challenges him to a duel *(ra).* Lorenzo enters the garden in response to the note he has received and, in the darkness, makes love to the maid Leonor believing her to be Isabel *(ra).* The Duke, too, arrives and enters the open door of the garden with the intention of identifying the lucky man who has gained entry *(ra).* Act I ends on this dramatically ironic note leaving the audience to wonder about the resolution of the situation.

Act II. Lorenzo, having enjoyed his dalliance with Leonor, runs into the Duke and, without having identified himself, agrees to a duel at the spot and time previously assigned for the duel with Cosimo *(ra).* There, Cosimo refuses to draw his sword on the Duke, offering his life, but when Alessandro tells him that the reason for his anger is that he believes Cosimo to have enjoyed Isabel's favors in the garden, his jealousy makes him flee, intent upon seeking her out to verify her apparent lack of honesty and honor *(ra).* Lorenzo asks Cefio for Isabel's hand and is refused. He then tells Cefio that he has already enjoyed her love, but to no avail since Cefio continues to refuse to accept the marriage. Lorenzo sees the Duke as the cause of his difficulties and decides to assassinate him when the opportunity arises *(ra)*. The Duke orders Lorenzo to seek out and kill Cosimo and tells him of his plans to get Isabel to the palace as lady-in-waiting to the Duchess Marie so that he can have access to her himself *(ra)*. Cosimo faces Isabel wanting to know about what had transpired in the garden. At last they are both convinced that these misunderstandings are the result of an evil plot hatched by the Duke and Lorenzo. After a scene of loving forgiveness, they promise to marry *(pp)*. Cefio returns and faces Isabel with Lorenzo's claims *(pt)*. She denies having been with him. Lorenzo arrives to tell them that the Duke is coming to take her to the palace and presses his own suit as a means of avoiding that danger *(pt)*. In a rapid series of scenes the various principals enter and speak. Different aspects of the predicament emerge in seeming opposition to each other. The poet succeeds in creating dramatic tension by skillfully handling the irony inherent to the circumstances, an irony that can be resolved only if the maid Leonor will tell the truth *(rt* and *pt)*. The second act concludes as Leonor again avoids the necessity for explanations.

Act III. Isabel, accompanied by Leonor, follows Cosimo to his refuge. She has escaped with the help of the Duchess whom she has told of the Duke's real reasons for bringing her to the palace. The people of Florence, she tells Cosimo, side with him *(rt)*. Just as Leonor admits barely enough of the truth (or another version of it) to satisfy the two and they reconcile, the Duke arrives, finds the pair together, and orders Cosimo's death as he, himself, chases after Isabel *(pt)*. The fleeing Cosimo runs into Lorenzo's servant Julio and gets another bit of the truth from him about what happened, just enough to overturn Leonor's last version *(pt)*. Then he finds another letter from Lorenzo, one to a co-conspirator that details a plot to kill Alessandro and take over the government of Florence *(rt)*. Cosimo responds to the call of duty once more by returning to Florence to give the alarm *(rt)*. The problem of Isabel is finally resolved as the whole truth comes out, Cosimo finds Lorenzo, too late, in a locked room with the body of Alessandro whom he had stabbed. He chases the escaping Lorenzo and kills him *(ec)*. Cosimo returns to take over the rule of Florence himself, obtains Cefio's permission for his marriage to Isabel, sends Leonor to a convent, and rewards all *(dt)*.

This *comedia* is based on historical circumstances tied to Spain's past through Charles V's involvement in Florentine politics. The author, in the final lines, refers to the historicity of the drama by calling it "The tragedy of Alessandro." It is noteworthy for its regularity of verse and structure, and especially for the poet's development of the technique of ending the first and second acts each with an unresolved climactic scene that demands and receives resolution in the opening scenes of the next act where he has the time and space to employ that completion as a springboard to the next problem. Also of great interest in this play is the careful manner in which the opposing characters of Cosimo and Lorenzo are drawn, and Enciso's masterful use of dramatic irony as he plays with the varying levels of knowledge held by the different characters and the audience.

Among other plays by Jiménez de Enciso that are well worth reading and study are his *El encubierto* [The Undercover Man],[22] a tale of the rebellion of the *comuneros* against the rule of Charles V under the leadership of a supposed cousin, the grandson of Ferdinand and Isabella through their son Juan. Juan died shortly after his marriage and although it was reported that the child resulting from that marriage had been a still-born girl, there were rumors that Philip, husband to Juana, who was to inherit the throne from her parents now that her brother Juan was dead, and the Cardinal Primate of Spain had conspired to hide the birth of a son, who became "El Encubierto." Enciso also wrote a *comedia* dealing with the retirement of the Emperor Charles V to Yuste, *La mayor hazaña de Carlos V* [The Greatest Deed of Charles V]. In this play dealing with Charles's penance and holy death, the structure is typically one of mirroring actions. One particularly interesting mirror scene is that which uses an exorcism as the basis for a comic action. Enciso's *Santa Margarita*[23] is the only one of the plays attributed to him without question that does not deal with royal history of the sixteenth century. This *comedia* is made up from the standard hagiographic stuff of a Christian virgin martyr in the Roman Empire of Diocletian. By means of her faith and her prayers, Margaret repeatedly saves herself from being raped by various Romans, the last of the series being the Emperor himself. This incident is in part an echo of the scene in Enciso's *Prince Charles* in which the Prince attempts sexual assault on the body of the Ambassador from Flanders. Here the blinded Emperor Diocletian, intent on attacking Margaret who is protected by her faith, charges into the theater audience searching for the lady whom he intends to rape. He finally runs into the *gracioso* (Tirso), who, after several hilarious references to himself as a bearded lady, demands that lights be brought in order to protect himself as well as other male victims from sexual assault.

In summary, Jiménez de Enciso was a careful playwright, one who showed the greatest interest in presenting historical drama. His use of such varied techniques for increasing audience awareness and participation in the plays as (1) a real mastery of the poetic language and structures of the *comedia*, (2) a careful choice of such dramatic materials as would arouse and titillate the public, (3) the development of situations aimed at carrying interest in the plot over from the end of one act to the beginning of the next, and (4) directly addressing the audience in ways that extended to the employment of the entire theater as an extension of the stage (Imagine audience reaction when the Emperor Diocletian runs out into the audience intent upon rape of the first victim who falls into his searching hands!), all these speak eloquently for recognition of the author as an inventive writer well acquainted with both the theater and the genre itself as a living art of action and reaction.

Luis de Belmonte Bermúdez (1587–1650?)

One of the dramatists of the decade who probably, as shown by the numerous texts he wrote in collaboration, had the greatest number of literary friends and admirers was Luis de Belmonte Bermúdez, who wrote somewhere between twenty and twenty-five extant *comedia* texts completely on his own. Born in Seville, as were Claramonte, Godínez, and Jiménez de Enciso, Belmonte went to the New World as a youth. There he undoubtedly wrote poetry and some drama during the first two decades of the century but, since he took part in the literary festivities of 1620 and 1622 in Madrid, we know he·was there when he wrote the play that I will discuss here: *El diablo predicador* [The Preacher Devil], performed in the Royal Palace in 1623. *El sastre del Campillo* [The Tailor from Campillo], another play of this period, can be dated in 1624, as can *La renegada de Valladolid* [The Lady Renegade from Valladolid]. Although these three must be considered his most important plays, we know that Belmonte continued to write plays until as late as 1641, when permission was given for a limited run of his *El acuerdo en el engaño* [Agreement about Deception] by the censor with some misgivings about the decency of the work. Here I wish to document Belmonte's mastery of the use of dramatic irony toward a comic end as well as his use of historical material to emphasize a theme, the theme of loyalty in this case. I am only partially in agreement with William Kincaid's assessment of the structure of his *comedias* when he claimed that "Most of Belmonte's dramas suffer from some serious weakness in construction. Besides anticipation of climax, his plays show generally lack of cohesion, and also contain a large amount of unrelated elements which tend to obscure the issue."[24] That opinion is one I find to be colored by outdated concepts of what dramatic structure should be, concepts that do not take into account the aesthetic principles operating at the time the *comedia* was formed as a literary genre.

The Preacher Devil.[25] Depending almost entirely on irony as a means of achieving both humor and comedy (humor results in laughter, comedy in pleasure), this play works only if the public before whom it is performed, or by whom it is read, comprehends the interoperation of the allegorical representation of a battle between the forces of good and evil as well as the legends of St. Francis that the author uses to construct a new mythology that must be perceived as both comic and serious in intent. This *comedia* is a quintessential representation of the Horatian precept demanding delightful utility, the *utile dulci.*

Act I. Lucifer flies onto the stage on the back of a dragon at the same time that Asmodeus emerges from a trap door. The two expose the situation existing in the Italian town of Lucca, where a rich and avaricious man, Louis, has arranged a marriage for himself with a poor but virtuous lady. Octavia had wanted to marry Felix but has dutifully accepted her father's wish that she marry Louis. Lucifer is determined to use Louis's avarice as a means for tempting a group of Franciscans trying to establish a convent in Lucca. It is Lucifer's hope that he will thus gain access to those Christian souls denied him through the steadfast faith and example of the friars *(ex)*. Felix appears at the home of Louis and Octavia to congratulate them and, in a series of speeches frought with ironic intent, the true situation becomes clear: Octavia still loves Felix. He still loves her. Octavia is unhappy but faithful in her marriage *(in)*. The Superior of the convent and Fray Tony, a lay brother, come to beg alms and are refused first by Louis and then by the other citizens of Lucca following his lead *(ra)*. St. Michael brings word to Lucifer that his machinations have offended God, since although he has God's permission to tempt the faithful he is not permitted to countermand a promise that God has already made: here God's promise to St. Francis that those faithful to his order will never go hungry. As punishment, Lucifer is ordered to take on the habit of the Order and to join the friars in their work as if he were St. Francis himself. Unwillingly, Lucifer does so taking the name Fray "Forced Obedience." As Fray Tony goes off with Lucifer to obtain food, he notes a definitely sulfurous air about the new friar *(ra)*.

Act II. After five months have passed, all the friars, exept for the Superior, who knows his identity, and Fr. Tony, who senses it, think of Fr. Obedience as a saint because of his superhuman efforts to build the new convent as well as carry on the work of the Order *(ra)*. Octavia rebuffs advances by Felix but their interview is witnessed by her husband who, his jealousy aroused, plots to kill her *(ra)*. Fr. Obedience lectures Louis on the dangers of his sinful course in a masterful display of irony and rhetoric but fails in his efforts to reduce the miser to penitence *(pp)*. Fr. Tony has escaped to the countryside with food and drink he hopes to enjoy, but Fr. Obedience comes and, in a scene reminiscent of the miracle of the loaves and fishes, all the food is given to needy people and Fr. Tony is left hungry and thirsty *(rt)*. Louis comes with Octavia, draws his sword, and, in spite of Fr. Obedience's interference, kills her *(pt)*. As Fr. Tony watches, Obedience waits to see what happens to Octavia's soul. The invisible Virgin Mary descends on a cloud and Octavia revives just as Felix comes on the scene *(rt)*. Even though death had released her from her marriage vows, Octavia refuses Felix, since to accept him now would lend credence to any doubts about her virtue *(pt)*.

Act III. Octavia, who has been staying in the country, decided that she will return to Louis and, if he will not have her, she will enter a convent *(pt)*. Fr. Tony enters running from a mob that, as a result of the distribution of his food that had seemed to be miraculous, thinks of him as a saint. Offered protection from the relic-seeking crowd as well as food and drink, he hesitatingly accepts, but Fr. Obedience stops him once again *(rt)*. Octavia leaves to return to Louis and is followed by the two friars. When she faces him, he refuses to accept her and again tries to kill her *(pt)*. This time Fr. Tony, pushed by Fr. Obedience, steps between them and he lectures Louis on his duties *(rt)*. Fr. Obedience sends his companion for the Superior and he, too, tries to convert Louis but again Louis's lack of faith keeps him from repenting his sins and he sinks into Hell still refusing to give alms *(ec)*. Lucifer calls forth Astaroth to take the form of Louis, give away the wealth, and then reveal his true identity. As Lucifer descends into Hell along with Astaroth, Octavia agrees to accept Felix as husband following a proper period of mourning for her dead husband *(dt)*.

This *comedia* is an important one for my present purposes since it contains several items of interest to the developing genre. At some point, the dramatists must have become aware of the prime importance of an opening scene as an attention getter. The first thing that happens onstage in this play is one clearly designed to capture the eye and mind of the public. Lucifer flies onto the stage on the back of a dragon. Because he calls up Asmodeus here, it also serves as a foreshadowing of the denouement preparing the audience for the calling up of Astaroth, thus avoiding a sense of *deus ex machina* at that moment. This opening scene also prepares the public to accept the various entries and exits made in the play via stage machinery *(tramoyas)*. Too, the play is structured in such a way that successive scenes serve as a thematic mirroring of each other: the obedient but unwilling wife Octavia mirrors the figure of Lucifer as he takes the name Fr. Forced Obedience. This comparison is underscored by repeated references to each one's unwillingness and obedience. Fray Tony, who throughout the play is the companion of Fray Obedience, is a gluttonous counterpart to the avaricious Louis, Octavia's husband. This mirrorlike doubling is constant throughout the work. Immediately following the scene, for example, in which Fr. Obedience lectures Louis on his avarice to reduce him to penitence, he lectures Fr. Tony on his gluttony, forcing him to distribute the food he has gathered for himself to the needy.

Two short exchanges will serve here to indicate the fashion in which Belmonte employs dramatic irony. (I feel a need here to remind the reader that my translations cannot do justice to the original). Ironic meaning often flits over the face of the speeches of the two friars. Fr. Tony tries to excuse his gluttony:

FR. TONY: The Devil makes me do it!
FR. OBEDIENCE: You lie!

It is your own weakness that causes it. Has
the Devil ever told you, even once in all the
times he's talked with you, that gluttony is
not a sin?

FR. TONY: No, but gluttony is the name given to eating
when you're not hungry. I'm always hungry.
(337c)

Each is telling the precise truth as he knows it, but the audience knows,
in addition, that Fr. Obedience *is* the devil as well as the fact that Fr.
Tony is the *gracioso*. (Here he is a combination of Flip Wilson and
Wimpy.) Just as the dramatist uses irony as a source of humor in the
preceding passage, he also uses it for comedy as in the scene in which
Felix comes to congratulate the newlyweds. The words spoken by Felix
and by Octavia carry a different message for each other and for the
audience from that which they carry for the avaricious bridegroom. (I
have enclosed the doubled meaning in parentheses.)

FELIX: Since until I saw her married (to another man), I had always
taken her for someone else (mine, not yours).
LOUIS: That's very odd.
OCTAVIA: My father's nature, as you know, was the cause (of my marriage).
FELIX: And your great (excessive) obedience! Enjoy Octavia, Louis,
throughout the years (very few!) that I wish for you both. (329a)

The passage continues in the same vein. The comedy in the situation
lies in the fact that the unhappy couple will eventually wind up married
to each other. The only structural weakness that I note in the play lies in
the many threads of plot that remain to be resolved following the
emotional climax of the work (Louis's descent into Hell): Lucifer's
resuscitation of Louis in the person of Astaroth in order to distribute the
ill-gotten wealth, the final open identification of Lucifer, and the
marriage of Felix and Octavia.

Lack of space here prohibits further study of Belmonte's many good
plays, even the two historically based works that are readily available.
In *The Tailor from Campillo*[26] Belmonte uses historical material to deal
with the theme of loyalty in a fine and varied study. The play approaches the subject dealing with the loyalty of (1) vassal to lord, (2) one
noble to another, (3) two friends, (4) a lady towards her intended

husband, (5) peasants to their masters, and, most interestingly, (6) the problem of divided loyalties. The other *comedia, The Lady Renegade from Valladolid,*[27] is also based on legendary materials. Isabela, at the last minute, deserts a religious life in the convent to run off with a handsome soldier. She and her husband are captured along with others when the Moors retake the fortress of Bujía in North Africa. Seeing her ill fortune to be a just punishment for her sinful act, she accepts Islam in order to marry the Moorish king, but then uses her power to free the Christian captives, to return to Spain and her own religion.

Both plays follow the pattern set in the *Preacher Devil* in making good use of the opening scene to get the attention of the audience. *The Tailor from Campillo* opens with Manrique de Lara rushing across the stage, a child on one arm, a sword in the other hand. He speaks just two short verses before leaving, others then enter to present the more standard expository material. He says, "I'm willing to die, if only you can be saved, Alphonse, King of Spain! (vv. 1–2)" (This King Alphonse is the same one whose later deeds were the subject of Lope de Vega's *Royal Reconciliation and Jewess of Toledo.*) *The Lady Renegade* opens when Isabela throws down a book, swearing to rid the house of all books dealing with devotional matters. Both plays utilize dramatic irony and the mirroring technique described above in dealing with the *Preacher Devil.*

A list of the other plays by Belmonte Bermúdez, too long to cite here, shows a strong preference for materials taken from Spanish history and a few on religious themes. There is a notable lack of the more standard "Cape and Sword" type of play as well as *comedias* based on the mythological subjects that were to become so important in the following decades (I have only been able to identify one play of the latter type).

Other Dramatists and Conclusion

There are, besides the three playwrights discussed here, at least twelve poets whose works belong primarily to this decade and whose plays I would recommend as worthy of study, but in the belief that the works and authors I have chosen to write about at length here are quite typical of the minor dramatists of the period, I leave to those interested the fascinating task of resuscitating their works for critical review. The are Juan Bautista Villegas, Antonio Sigler de la Huerta, Diego Muget y Solís, Gabriel del Corral, Juan Cabezas, Alonso de Osuna, Matías de los Reyes, Vicente Esquerdo, Rodrigo de Herrera, Jerónimo de Villaizán, and the two who are better known for the novels into which they intercalated their plays, Alonso Jerónimo de Salas Barbadillo and Alonso del Castillo Solórzano.

In summarizing what the works of these "minor" dramatists show us about the theater of the decade 1621–1630, I would like to indicate the following aspects as being the most noteworthy contributions made by them as they reflected the works of the major dramatists who were their competitors, perhaps even emphasizing the advances made by them or introducing new techniques of their own: (1) These dramatists as a group show a strong interest in portraying traditional tales based on Spanish history. In doing so, they demonstrate that they have learned to avoid the linear, pageant-type structures employed by the earlier dramatists. The primary technique for doing so is to employ a parallel love intrigue in such a way as to mirror the dramatic thesis at the center of the basic theme. (2) The ability of these dramatists to adapt their materials to basic dramatic structures (exposition, initiating incident, rising action or plot complication, pivotal or turning point, tensing action, emotional climax, and denouement) is remarkable in that they almost invariably follow that set pattern. (3) The playwrights of this decade certainly paid attention, and close attention, to the working of the drama as a theatrical experience, as is shown by the care they took in exciting audience interest and participation through active opening scenes, unresolved climactic act endings, the judicious use of stage machinery, and the careful choice of interesting subject matter. (4) The increasingly difficult poetic language through which the actors projected their characters bespeaks an audience well prepared through constant contact with the genre to accept this aspect as one more of those theatrical conventions the acceptance of which leads to the "suspension of disbelief" so necessary to a working theater. (5) Another technique that was increasingly mastered by the poets was dramatic irony (deceiving with the truth) so well employed earlier—Lope de Vega insists invented—by Miguel Sánchez. This technique they used with an increasingly delicate touch as they learned to handle it more carefully and became more fully aware of the possibilities of using levels of meaning that varied with the point of view of the characters speaking and the listening public. Finally (6), acceptance by the audience of the didacticism that is so apparent in the plays of this decade was a necessary ingredient in the eventual conquest of the principle of *utile dulci,* which is so easily recognized in the overwhelming importance placed on the thesis of the works prepared in this period, and the constant use of contemporary political and literary satire in the mouth of the *gracioso,* the standard figure of wit.

Chapter Four
Calderón's Competitors (1631–1650)

The twenty-year period from 1631 to 1650 has long been recognized as centering about the second of the two masters of the Spanish Golden Age drama, Pedro Calderón de la Barca. Although this oversimplified compartmentalization of the literary history of the theater is often, and quite correctly, criticized, I find it a useful device to employ in studying the stylistic and structural changes that took place in the *comedia* between the earliest years of the seventeenth century and these middle years of concern to us here. That this was truly an era of Calderonian hegemony is demonstrated in part by the fact that Lope de Vega himself, in the plays he wrote during the last years of his life (1631–1635), was greatly influenced by the changes in the *comedia* format developed in the works of the Calderonian dramatists as well as in those transitional writers of the preceding decade: (1) a simpler, more unified structure in which the lines dividing plot from subplot become so diffused as to make recognition of them as separate entities difficult; (2) a richer, more cultivated poetic vocabulary reflecting the influence on the language of the great Baroque poets; (3) a more finely honed sense of character in the plays, characterization that is to be perceived in the audience reaction to and identification with the stage personalities being portrayed; and (4) a more serious approach to the drama that is best evidenced by the deepened thematic meaning expressed through the action of the plays. Among Lope de Vega's *comedias* of this period are three well-known works that exhibit these qualities to a striking degree when compared to his earlier plays: *El castigo sin venganza* [Punishment without Revenge], *Las bizarrías de Belisa* [Belisa's Generosity], and *El amor enamorado* [Love in Love].[1]

A second element inherent to the labeling of this period as Calderonian is found in the figures for the number of plays that Calderón composed during the years concerned. No other dramatists of the period wrote as many of the extant texts as did Calderón. Of the *comedias* we have from his hand, fifteen were probably written before 1631 for an average of one and one-half plays per year in the third decade of the poet's life. The two decades 1631 to 1650 saw the preparation of between sixty and sixty–five of the extant plays, an average of more than three per year. In the last thirty years of his life (1651–1681), Calderón seems to have produced no more than thirty-five to forty plays, only slightly more than one *comedia* per year. That this is not due to mere lack of creative energy is shown by the fact that this same period witnessed the writing of fifty-one of the seventy-one *autos sacramentales* (one-act Eucharistic allegories) that he wrote.[2] There were other reasons, as well, for the reduction in Calderón's productivity in the field of the *comedia* as I shall show below.

One well-known dramatist whose works are generally thought of as representative of the "Calderonian cycle" is Juan Pérez de Montalván (1601–1638),[3] who is also known as a younger friend and admirer of Lope de Vega. In her study of Montalván, Maria Grazia Profeti makes a strong case for recognizing him as a dramatist of the transition from Lopean to Calderonian drama. Profeti shows clearly that Montalván cannot be considered a mere follower of Lope since he does not slavishly follow that master's lead. She also claims that he followed Calderón in the use of such dramatic techniques as repeated motifs and paralleled mirroring situations.[4] I would only add here that even though it is my belief that Calderón himself was following the lead of the dramatists of the 1620s, who were indeed the "transitional" artists, the importance of the matter lies in the fact that those techniques came to be tied to Calderón's name as elements typical of his works.

Another of the principal writers of the period was certainly Luis Vélez de Guevara (1579–1644), who wrote a large number of his *comedias* precisely during the period that concerns us here. He is, perhaps, best recognized as the author of the satiric picaresque novel *El diablo cojuelo* [The Limping Devil] of 1641, yet he is also important for his dramatic works. These have been often spoken of as works of pomp and circumstance and were popular both in the court and in the public theaters because of the violent action and brilliant visual effects so typical of them.[5]

The third of the important dramatists of the Calderonian group was Francisco de Rojas Zorrilla (1607–1648). Of him Raymond R. Mac-Curdy writes, "Rojas learned much of his craftsmanship from Vélez and Calderón, and although he continued to collaborate with the author of *La vida es sueño* [Life Is a Dream], he was soon vying with him for favor in the public theater and at the court."[6] Zorrilla is most important for two contributions he is said to have made to the development of the *comedia*. He worked at developing the role of the *gracioso,* often turning him into a main element of the play's intrigue. This led finally to making the humorous character the central figure of the play, a play in which the author studies the foibles of a central personage in what became known as the *comedia de figurón* (a play that is a study of an eccentric character). Again I would like to caution against hasty recognition of any single dramatist as the originator of a trend that is better understood as the result of a logical evolutionary process taking place in the works of many.[7]

Another dramatist of this period whose work must be recognized here is Antonio Enríquez Gómez, the second of the dramatists condemned by the Inquisition as a backsliding convert from Judaism who, as Fernando de Zárate (alias as well as pseudonym), witnessed his own execution, in effigy, in Seville in 1660.[8]

The theater of the period, too, was strongly affected by events outside the literary world that produced the texts. There are strong indications that court politics played a role in the type and number of plays prepared for performance at the court. Those courtiers who surrounded the Queen, for example, were anxious to support her in her own interests, interests that at times ran counter to those of the King's favorite, the Count-Duke of Olivares. Although Olivares was the real center of political power until his downfall in 1643, Philip IV did pay closer attention to affairs of state than he is generally given credit for. Obviously Olivares's own interest in and support of the theater was due, in part, to his wish to distract the King from royal duties, leaving the real (and more profitable) power to those including Olivares who were more willing to wield it.[9]

Important changes were occurring in the theatrical world as well. The Italian stage designer Cosme Lotti arrived in Madrid in 1626 and immediately we find plays requiring more elaborate settings and stage machinery, particularly for those works performed at the court theater in the Alcázar of Madrid. In 1629 Olivares began overseeing the planning and construction of the new palace at the Buen Retiro. By 1633 and 1634 the theater there was ready for performances. In addition to the theater itself, Lotti had so designed the royal gardens that plays could be performed at various locations: the tennis courts, the artificial lake, etc. We know also that Lotti worked in close collaboration with poets in planning plays around the machines and staging that he was able to design and build. Another notable change affecting the *comedias* written for palace performance was that plays came to be performed indoors at night on a stage that allowed for instantaneous scene changes. In 1640 the Coliseo at the Buen Retiro was opened and, for the first time, the royal theater and its attendant spectacle were open to the paying public. This was done as much to bring the atmosphere of the public *corral* to the palace for the amusement of the King and Queen as it was to open the palace for the amusement of the public.[10]

Lotti died in 1643, the same year that saw Olivares's downfall. Neither of these events had quite the same disastrous effect on the theater as did the death of the Queen in 1644. All theaters were ordered closed for a period of mourning that year. When Prince Baltasar Carlos died in 1646, the theaters were again closed. Although court festivities began again in December 1647, the public theaters remained closed until 1649 and many companies of actors disbanded as their members sought other employment. It was not until the arrival of the new Queen in December of 1649, not really until Carnival of 1650, that performances again began in earnest. In fact because of needed repairs, the Coliseo was not reopened to the public until 1651.[11] All of these matters must be considered in trying to realize the changes that took place in the drama (in its literary form) during that period. Certainly it is clear that the events that brought on the sporadic closing of the theaters resulted in a consequent real break in the continuity of theatrical history during the closing years of the decade of the forties.

Besides six lesser figures,[12] there are two dramatists whose works typify the theatrical fashions of this twenty-year span: Antonio Hurtado de Mendoza, the ultimate courtier and true opportunist, and Alvaro Cubillo de Aragón, who would have liked to belong to that select group but whose works were mainly performed for the paying public.

Antonio Hurtado de Mendoza (1586–1644)

Even though Antonio Hurtado de Mendoza's work as inventor of the infamous *papel sellado* (stamp-taxed paper used for legal matters) has undoubtedly affected the lives of more Spanish-speaking people than has his work as a dramatist, he is not unworthy of study as a poet and writer of *comedias*. [13] As a member of one of Spain's foremost families, although sprouted from a lesser branch, Antonio Mendoza was destined to take an active part in the court and in the literary circles of Madrid from the earliest years of the seventeenth century until his death. As a young man he was a friend of both Lope de Vega and Luis Vélez de Guevara. He served as godfather to one of Lope's illegitimate children in 1607 and he wrote an introductory sonnet for a volume of Vélez's work published in 1608. Even at this early date his propensity for making friends on both sides of a fence, literary or political, was obvious. When the Duke of Lerma fell in disgrace during the final years of the reign of Philip III, Mendoza saved himself from the political wreckage that was to cost other literary figures dearly by allying himself with the faction of Gaspar de Guzmán, the future Count-Duke of Olivares. It was very shortly after Olivares rose to power (March 1621) at the court of Philip IV that Mendoza entered the palace service (May 1621). He was promoted again in August of that year, became secretary to the King in March 1623, and married very well in July 1623 (a second marriage in 1631 was even more advantageous). In September 1623 he was made a knight of the Order of Calatrava, and in 1625 he was named secretary to the Holy Office (the Inquisition). While at the court, Mendoza seems to have been quite capable of walking the political tightrope between opposing factions. He was made Secretary of Justice by the King in 1641, yet when the Count-Duke fell in 1643, Mendoza did not follow him into disgrace but actually received a raise in salary. He died while on a visit to Zaragoza in 1644.

The dramatic piece that probably gained him most favor, one published complete with his own detailed description of its presentation at the summer palace in Aranjuez in 1622, was *Querer por sólo querer* [To Love for Love's Sake]. The piece falls outside our area of interest for reasons other than chronological. It was, as Mendoza himself says, not a *comedia* at all but rather an "invention" or court spectacle. The text is more than double the length normally expected of a *comedia* and deals with the chivalric, pastoral, and supernatural worlds. Gareth Davies says of the piece, "It would be wrong in this instance to talk of Wagnerian synaesthesia, but it is worth remembering that, in *Querer* itself, as in the other palace spectacles, the overall aim was a totality of effect, in which the senses, ambiguously and ambivalently stimulated, enriched the artistic impression conveyed by painter, poet, and musician."[14] The true *comedias* we have from Mendoza's pen, written during the early 1620s, are relatively poor stuff indeed when compared to the three later pieces that I wish to discuss here, yet they all show a very real lyric talent, a ready and cynical wit, and a willingness to attack the standard theatrical conventions of the period in an innovative fashion.

   Cada loco con su tema [Everyone is Crazy on Some Point].[15]   This play has been called one of the jewels of the Spanish Golden Age theater because of its intensely witty dialogue. It is an extremely funny comedy of action yet since, as the title indicates, it centers around the eccentricities of its various characters, it approaches the *comedia de figurón*. Gareth Davies believes the play to have been written originally in the early 1620s but to have been reworked for presentation in 1630, the date of the autograph manuscript. I find this difficult to accept since Davies offers no proof other than a reference to a play by that title with nothing to indicate that it refers to a work written by Mendoza.[16] Clearly, however, the play as we have it now belongs to the decades of interest here.

   Built around the theme expressed in its title, the play deals with the story of Hernán Pérez, recently returned from Peru where he has made himself wealthy. He has two marriageable daughters, Leonor and Isabel. Since he wants a kinsman to inherit his wealth, thus reestablishing the family in property as well as nobility, he insists on marrying one of them to a nephew. The girls have other ideas.

   Act I. The play gets off to a rousing start as Hernán Pérez chases the two girls onto the stage, threatening them with a rigorous caning unless one agrees to marry the man of his choosing, the cousin spoken of as *Montañés* ("Mountain Man"). The name refers not only to his position in society as a member of the old nobility but also to his physical size *(in)*. Isabel insists that she will marry only a man who is to her own taste—handsome; Leonor wants to marry for comfort—wealth. The girls are protected and abetted by their chaperone-aunt Aldonza who has not yet given up the search for a husband of her own. Isabel has left behind in Peru a suitor, Luis, a cousin on the maternal side of the family, but here in Spain has been eyeing a handsome young blade, Juan. Leonor has set her cap for the wealthy but eccentric Julián *(ex)*. While waiting in front of the church for the young ladies to appear, Juan urges his aide Bernardo to distract the aunt from her duties by making love to her. As Juan and Bernardo move off to one side, Julián enters with his servant and the two suitors size each other up from opposite sides of the stage. The ladies enter and the young men make them the center of their attention *(ra)*. Leonor drops her handkerchief, hoping that Julián will retrieve it, but he refuses to stoop and Juan returns it to Leonor, much to Isabel's jealous consternation. They all go off in their various directions *(ra)*. The father, at home waiting for the arrival of Montañés, is greeted by Luis. He tells Luis that Isabel is to marry her other cousin, the one from the mountains *(ra)*. Isabel, having heard of Luis's arrival, comes to greet him but runs, instead, into Montañés. She is horrified by his rough appearance as well as by his obviously uncultured manners *(ra)*. Luis and Montañés size each other up and agree to a duel to settle matters *(ra)*.

Act II. Luis and Montañés meet for their duel as first Juan and Bernard, then Julián and his servant, and finally Hernán Pérez and an old servant enter. All comment on the swordsmanship of the two fencers *(ra)*. When the two realize that they are cousins, if only by marriage, the duel stops, leaving both with slight wounds. The father goes off with Montañés *(ra)*. Luis is aided by Juan and the two become friends even though they are both interested in Isabel *(ra)*. The girls are introduced to their cousin from the mountains and he announces Isabel as his choice for a bride *(ra)*. As they start to embrace, signaling their acceptance of the engagement (Isabel quite unwillingly but obediently), Juan interrupts with a story about the wounds suffered by Luis. In a successful attempt to get Montañés out of the house and away from Isabel, he says that Luis has been questioned by the authorities about the illegal duel. Montañés goes off to seek asylum *(pp)*. Juan then tells Isabel that Luis's wounds were indeed slight. Her obvious relief at this news piques Juan's jealousy, so in order to get even with her, he pretends interest in Leonor *(pt)*. When Luis comes in, Juan tells him that Montañés was seriously wounded and that the law is after him. Luis, too, leaves to seek asylum *(rt)*. Julián enters and Isabel flirts with him hoping to make Juan jealous *(pt)*. Juan then pleads with Isabel to agree to marry him even though he cannot financially back a suit to force her father to recognize their right to marry *(rt)*. When Julián appears that evening with musicians to serenade Isabel, only the old servant man goes to the window. He, hoping to have fun with the eccentric Julián, pretends to be Isabel and agrees to marry Julián. This promise is witnessed by Juan who is also under the impression that the figure at the window is Isabel *(pt)*.

Act III. Hernán Pérez lectures his nephew on the proper manners and dress for a lover *(rt)*. An interview is arranged for Isabel and her cousin but it goes badly. He leaves, making it clear that he has changed his mind and now wants to marry Leonor instead *(rt)*. Juan and Isabel finally agree that they are indeed in love, but he wants her to think seriously about what they are doing; annoyed at his hesitation, she leaves *(pt)*. When Julián is caught by Montañés talking to Leonor, he runs away. Luis comes in and he and Montañés discover that the business about the wounds and the authorities being after them was not true. The two become friends and agree not to quarrel over the two girls *(pt)*. This is overheard by Isabel, who, in view of the lack of strong feeling on Luis's part, finally tells her father that she loves Juan and has already given herself to him sexually in anticipation of their marriage. Her father, necessarily, agrees to their marriage. In fact, he insists upon it. Just as Juan and Isabel are beginning to get things straight, everyone else enters *(dc)*. Montañés agrees to marry Leonor.[17] Julián interrupts, claiming that Isabel had already accepted him. They all have a hearty laugh as the old servant admits that it was he rather than Isabel at the window and that he, not Isabel, had promised to marry Julián *(dt)*.

The plot begins with Hernán's insistance on marrying one of his daughters to her cousin, a representative of the "old-Christian" branch of the family. The turning point or dramatic climax comes about when Juan successfully prevents that marriage from occurring at that time. The third key point, the emotional climax, certainly comes about when the young couple succeed in getting her father to agree to their marriage. The whole is thematically unified, as indicated in the title, by the monomania of each character. Hernán Pérez's single purpose is to restore social prestige to his family by marrying his wealth and daughter to a poor, but steady, cousin. Leonor wants to marry for wealth and comfort. Isabel desires a physically attractive husband. Each of the suitors, from the silly, foppish Julián to the rustic, untutored Montañés, is eccentric in his own way. At its best, the play makes an interesting, intelligent study of the characters, each of whom is dominated by a single purpose in life and subjects his actions to the accomplishment of that goal.

This work, structurally a rather typical novelesque cape and sword *comedia* set in a contemporary time period, deals with a familiar problem of the developing middle class of seventeenth-century Spain: the desire of the colonials, who returned to the mother land with wealth, to win social acceptance and to establish their families in society. Thus, the work is an early example of what might best be termed social comedy, another example of which is Mendoza's play *Los empeños del mentir* [The Trouble with Lying], structured around a picaresque theme.

The Trouble with Lying.[18]   In this self-conscious *comedia,* the text of which is laden with references not only to the genre but to the play itself, we find the author making use of the Spanish picaresque tradition in order to write a satirical social comedy. Here Mendoza makes use of the materials of Spain's great satirical genre to spoof the social climbers that swelled the ranks of the capital city's populace. This *comedia* was written, as comments within the text tell us, for performance at a celebration to be held at the Buen Retiro (thus after 1633). According to these comments, the piece was written by a gentleman (*hidalgo*) who has taken to writing *comedias* late in his life and against his will (452a).

Act I. Teodoro and Marcelo, two rogues, enter the city of Madrid through the Alcalá Gate, marveling at the sights: the Buen Retiro and the Prado. As they discuss the possibilities for getting on in this great city, they put on their spurs so that it will seem that they have ridden into town rather than walked. By chance they happen upon a man, Diego, who is being attacked by three thieves. They go to his rescue *(in)*. When Diego asks them who they are, they counter by questioning him *(ra)*. He gives his name and tells them that his father had come to

Madrid seeking reward for services as a soldier and that his brother Pedro had recently been killed in battle in Alsace. The pair pick up this lead and claim to have served with Pedro there. Diego then asks if they know Luis de Vivero, a young man whom Pedro had recommended for marriage to their sister Elvira. Marcelo claims to be that same Luis and the two are invited home with Diego *(ra)*. Elvira and her cousin Ana are surprised when Diego enters with her husband-to-be, whose appearance, to say the least, is not to Elvira's liking. She asks Ana's help in avoiding such a marriage *(ra)*. Teodoro, upset because Marcelo had got in first with the key lie, allows himself to be overheard promising Marcelo that he plans to "tell all" *(ra)*.

Act II. This leads everyone to believe that Teodoro is the real "Luis," a "fact" that he finally admits, claiming to have wanted to study the bride-to-be while still incognito *(ra)*. Even though Teodoro is physically more to Elvira's liking, she is not easily convinced in spite of Diego's pushing for an immediate wedding *(ra)*. Teodoro almost convinces them all of his identity with a tremendous, lying narrative description of the battle of Nordlingen that Marcelo comments on, in an aside, as a masterful lie since it contains so much truth *(pp)*. Elvira overhears the two rogues as they plot further action, but when she faces them *(rt)*, Marcelo suddenly addresses Teodoro as "Count Fabio," son of the "Marquis of Bitoldo," threatening to return to Italy to tell his father of where he, Fabio, has been hiding out in an effort to escape marriage to the Viceroy's daughter. Elvira promises to keep their secret (while she checks into this story), since she does not want to lose such an advantageous marriage for herself if the identification is a real one this time *(pt)*. Even Elvira's maid, Teresa, plays the social-climbing game as she asks Marcelo whether or not the maids of countesses are true ladies. She hopes to back the marriage to "Count Fabio" as a means of raising her own social station. Elvira, in the meantime, hopes to find out the truth of the matter before taking any unrevokable steps *(rt)*.

Act III. Diego who has been offered the prospect of marriage to the noble sister of "Count Fabio," is quite as easily convinced of this latest self-promotion as he was of the earlier lies *(pt)*. But Elvira takes advantage of an opportunity to search through the belongings of the "Count" *(rt)*, where she, of course, finds "proof" of his background. Diego now insists on an immediate wedding. Even Ana and Teresa are persuaded at this point, but Elvira still has doubts *(pt)*. All is going well for the *pícaros* until the real Luis de Viveros arrives *(rt)*. They attempt to brazen it out by accusing him as a thief who has stolen their jewels and papers. When the goods are found in Luis's things, Diego in view of his social position, places him under house arrest *(pt)*. First Elvira and then Teodoro offer him a chance to escape, but Luis refuses until justice has been done *(rt)*. The emotional climax of the piece occurs when two captains and several servants who have been with Luis arrive to identify him, thus bringing about the downfall of the rogues *(ec)* who finally admit the truth of the matter and go off to Flanders in the hope of bettering themselves there. Luis accepts marriage to Elvira and Diego marries Ana, while Teresa is left without a husband *(dt)*.

The self-conscious nature of this play is noticed not only where the piece speaks of its own performance, but throughout the work. For example: (1) Teresa, when she sees Marcelo as the proposed husband for Elvira, remarks in an aside that even in a *comedia* she would not accept a man such as he. (2) Elvira, when she is told that Teodoro is the "real Luis," says that nothing of this business has the ring of truth to it since what has happened seems to be impossible and foolish, even if pleasant, just as in a *comedia*. (3) When Teodoro relates the story of the battle of Nordlingen, Diego admiringly states his conviction that here, indeed, is a real Spaniard, one to whom any princess would be happy to attach herself without fear of the stain of theatrical sin. (4) At the point of highest emotional tension, the imminent arrival of Luis's people who will prove his identity. Marcelo remarks on the seeming impossibility of winding up so many plot threads in a single play and offers the audience a second part in which to do so. (5) Teodoro's final justification of his lies, spoken as he leaves for Flanders, is that the whole world is a theater in which all act (or lie) their parts. And (6), at the very end, when Teresa is asked why she too is not getting married, she complains that since the play has no lackey, there is no one in it for her to marry.

In addition to the apparent awareness of its own existence as a genre, the play shows a particularly strong consciousness of itself as a piece of literature within a literary body. This intertextuality is of a type certain to be most appreciated by the culturally aware audience it would have had at the Buen Retiro. As examples I would cite the reference noted above to "theatrical sin" in phraseology paralleling references to original sin (Mendoza had used this same type of reference earlier in *Everyone Is Crazy* when he wrote of Montañés, who had failed to remove his hat, as having been conceived in original *hat*). In *The Trouble with Lying,* he also refers to ballads from Spanish tradition, contemporary authors, and, at the conclusion makes use of a twisted theatrical cliché that has a wealth of possible related interpretations: "Let him who has believed all this pay for it" *(Quien tal habló, que tal pague).*

The work is truly a satiric social *comedia* dealing with and poking fun at the hordes of social climbers that infested Madrid's society in which each person was out to lift himself to higher rank by any means at his disposal. The women of this play, Elvira, Ana, and even the maid Teresa, are all willing to give up a marriage for love if they can make a socially advantageous match. It is Elvira's good sense and careful skepticism that prevails at the end. Her gullible brother continually attempts to force her to go against what her common sense tells her is correct. The two opportunistic *pícaros* unashamedly use every means at hand to try to get ahead. In the entire cast, only Luis, a stock-figure type rather than a real character, is not painted as a social climber. Since he is important to the play only to bring it to a close, the work resolves itself into a character study and satire of those who have come to Madrid in order to get ahead in life.

El marido hace mujer [The Husband Makes the Wife].[19]   As Gareth Davies notes, Mendoza's center of concern in this *comedia,* another that might also be called a social drama, is the husband-wife relationship in marriage, an institution he views as a social bond, rather than a sacrament, that may break when overstrained.[20] Again, in this work, Mendoza employs a theatrical cliché against which to react as a means of structuring his play: the conventional multiple marriage that normally concludes a *comedia.* Rather than end the play in this manner, he begins it with the celebration of a double wedding and then turns to what happens thereafter for the material from which to build his drama in a symmetrically arranged, nearly antiphonal fashion.

Act I. To the accompaniment of much comic banter on the part of the servants Morón an Inés (about the joys and tribulations of the married state), the wedding party returns home. The brothers Juan and Sancho, at the behest of their uncle Fernando, have married sisters, Leonor and Juana. Inés, Leonor's maid, passes a note to Morón, servant to Diego, Leonor's former gallant *(in)*. When the brides are left alone for a moment together, Juana, who has married Sancho, self-righteously declares her decision to accept the duty and to endure the suffering indicated by her new status. She intends to subject herself completely to the will and demands of her new husband. On the other hand, Leonor sees marriage as a means for achieving freedom from the constraints imposed by the need to guard her virginity from any taint of gossip. She will give her husband as good as he sends. For her, marriage is a two-way street that she intends to travel for her own benefit and happiness *(ex)*. The bridegrooms, too, differ in their approach. Sancho, who is every bit as unbending and puritanical as is his bride, intends to lay down the law to her and to tighten the chains binding her as a necessary means for guarding his own honor. He will do this even before sitting down to their wedding supper *(ex)*. Juan, on the other hand, warns his brother that to tell a bride what she *may* not do is to let her know what she *can* do. He preaches trust and love as the proper way of treating one's wife *(ex)*. Juan goes off to supper and to bed *(ra)*. When Diego comes to the house, ostensibly to help celebrate the wedding, Juan welcomes him politely but lets him know that the party is over. Sancho is both rude and jealous in attempting to eject him *(ra)*.

Act II. The brothers Sancho and Juan catch Diego's servant Morón with a love note. Juan reads it and returns it to Morón with orders to deliver it as intended *(ra)*. Sancho is sure that his brother is covering up for Juana. Juan, having read the letter, knows that it was intended for his own wife Leonor but takes this means to avoid scandal. Juan then tells Leonor that he and Sancho had intercepted a letter and about Sancho's jealousy. Avoiding an accusation, he tells her that he is pleased not to have any reason to deal with her as Sancho does with his wife *(ra)*. As Leonor prepares for an outing on the Calle Mayor, Juana enters. They quarrel when Juana questions the propriety of Leonor's going out, even when accompanied by Inés. Sancho and Juan enter. Sancho asks where the ladies are going. Juan insists that it is their business. Sancho forbids Juana to leave. Juan requests that she accompany Leonor on the outing *(ra)*. Left alone, the ladies make a choice. Leonor, in response to Juan's trust in her, stays home. Juana, angered by Sancho's mistrust, borrows Leonor's *manto* (the long, opaque covering worn by Madrilenian ladies of the period whenever leaving the house) and she goes out to the Calle Mayor *(pp)*. While walking along the street Juana meets and talks with Diego who decides to pursue her rather than Leonor *(pt)*. Sancho, sure that the lady talking with Diego is his sister-in-law, tells Juan about the pair. Juan refuses to listen to such gossip even from a brother *(rt)*. In an ironic scene, Sancho, upset by his brother's seeming indifference to the situation, tells the lady just what he would do to her if she were his wife. She is! *(pt)*.

Act III. When Juan returns home, ready to wreak vengeance for his lost honor on his wife, providing the proof of her infidelity is complete and he can do so without arousing further gossip, he finds that she had been home all the time and praises her for her loyalty to him *(rt)*. Juana then returns and is lectured by Leonor, but she is in no mood to accept the proffered advice or even to award Sancho the title of husband *(rt)*. Sancho finds his wife, Juana, at home, but rather than find reason for trust, he blames her for having allowed Leonor to go out. She asks him what seems to be a rhetorical question but is the ironic truth (443a): Wouldn't it have been much worse if it were I talking [to a man] on the Calle Mayor and my own husband were to have seen it? *(pt)*. Diego comes in response to an invitation from Juana but is told by Inés that Leonor has used her sister's name and he is talking to her in the dark. Juan overhears Diego talking to a lady whom he calls Leonor, telling her that he no longer has any interest in her and that she should be grateful for the fine husband she already has *(pt)*. Rather than attack immediately, Juan waits to hear the confirming tones of his wife's voice before killing the pair. The lady clears all up for him when she declares herself to be, indeed, Juana *(rt)*. Sancho enters, too, in the dark, and there is great confusion until Fernando comes in with lights *(ec)*. Convinced, at last, of Sancho's irremediable foolishness, Fernando announces that he will seek an immediate annulment for the match. Sancho realizes his error but also that he cannot change his ways, so the marriage is broken *(dt)*.

Again the author has offered what is best described as a social comedy, one in which he effectively employs the wise, measured reactions of the husband Juan to situations, that in too many other *comedias* of the time led to that bloody vengeance that is always tied to Spanish "honor" dramas, to contrast with the foolish actions and reactions of the jealous, domineering husband Sancho. Not only does the play, then, react against the multitude of *comedias* that end with the marriage of happy couples but against the very motif that informs it. In doing so, the poet presents us with a constant, running series of comic comments on the marriage relationship through the mouth of the *gracioso* Morón, whose first lines ask for a reward in exchange for his bringing the good news that since there is such a good crop of fools this year, there will be husbands for all (421a). He ends the play commenting to the audience that they will have to admit that since the work ends with an annulment, it ends well (436c).

Antonio Hurtado de Mendoza, palace poet, must be recognized as an important dramatist even if an unwilling one (as he himself claims), because his very few plays are indicative of a new direction, and yet they fit well within the generic mold. The plays discussed here are among his more original offerings but others of his *comedias* do offer evidence of a continuing interest in the foibles and problems of contemporary society. Occasionally characters within the works (characterization is one of his strong points) approach the stature of a *figurón,* yet his plays never really depend on that type of exaggerated character as do some later plays. The language used by Mendoza is literate but is neither objectionably abstruse nor stilted. The structures he employs are simple, yet the surface of the plays is covered with the complicated and fast moving action that is typical of the best *comedias.* He is quite self-consciously different in the topics he selects as subjects for his plays: (1) The wealthy *indianos* (colonials) who seek to use their wealth to "reestablish" a social position for a family that never truly had one. (2) The pressures on those who want to improve their social status by going to Madrid for the purpose of climbing the social ladder. (In *The Trouble with Lying,* the audience finds it hard not to feel just as sympathetic, if not more so toward the openly picaresque liars as with the more "regular" social climbing characters of the play.) (3) The problems of a marriage relationship in a real-life situation, problems that begin with the wedding rather than end there.

Of particular note is Mendoza's awareness, at all times, of the fact that he is presenting *comedia.* He constantly reminds the audience of that fact (as noted above). Another prime example of this tendency is found in his earlier play *No hay amor donde hay agravio* [There Can Be No Love Where There Is an Offense].[21] The *gracioso* finds himself in a position where he would like to react bravely and come to the aid of his master, but he cannot do so since the poet who is writing the play has no right to change the rules for such characters (fol. 26r.) Other plays by Mendoza include *Celos sin saber de quien* [Jealousy, But of Whom?], *Más merece quien más ama*[He Who Loves Best Deserves More], *Los riesqos que tiene un coche*[The Risks of a Coach], *El galán sin dama* [The Gallant without a Lady], and *El premio de la virtud* [The Reward of Virtue].[22] In addition to several plays that have been lost but which Mendoza is known to have authored,[23] there is an unedited manuscript found in the Barberini collection of the Vatican Library of a play, *Ni callarlo ni decirlo* [Neither to Say It Nor to Keep Quiet About It] that is attributed to him.[24]

Alvaro Cubillo de Aragón (1596–1661)

As Shirley Whitaker shows in her monographic study of Alvaro Cubillo de Aragón,[25] he did not arrive in Madrid from his home city of Granada until well after his reputation as a dramatist had been established. Although several of his works were performed at the court in the mid-1630s, Cubillo was then still living in Granada, where he earned his living as a judicial secretary *(escribano)*. By 1641 he had arrived in Madrid, where he continued in the same type of post, working for the city government *(ayuntamiento)* until his death in 1661.

Fully half of the twenty-six *comedia* texts we have from his hand are based on stories from Spanish history and national legend. Of these thirteen plays, all but three are reworkings, in one way or another, of earlier *comedias.* Cubillo joins Moreto, then, in the wholesale rewriting of earlier works, occasionally quite successfully eliminating episodes extraneous to the drama, strengthening the structural force of the play, or developing the characterization of the protagonist in tune with the aesthetic of the period in which he was working. Probably the best of these reworkings, certainly the most frequently read, performed, and criticized, is his dyptich on Bernardo del Carpio; the two parts of *El Conde de Saldaña.*[26]

Besides historico-legendary plays, Cubillo also tried his hand at religious drama. We have the texts of six of them. Of the two Old Testament plays, *El justo Lot* [Lot the Just], and *El mejor rey del mundo*

[The Best King in the World],[27] the first deals, of course, with the destruction of Sodom and Gomorrah and the second with Solomon and the Queen of Sheba. Both are episodic pageants in format, clearly designed to delight the eye of the public. The same is true of his quite unusual *Los triunfos de San Miguel* [The Triumphs of St. Michael],[28] in which he reworks three earlier *comedias,* one for each act, to portray St. Michael as the champion of mankind in his battle against Satan. The first act depends on Lope de Vega's *La creación del mundo y primera culpa de Adán* [Creation of the World and Adam's First Sin] not only for the Cain-Abel theme but also for the depiction of the struggle between Lucifer and St. Michael. The second act seems related to Claramonte's *The Godless City* (see Chapter 2) for the depiction of sinful Nineveh and the fulminations of Jonah. Act III turns again to Lope de Vega and his play on the Visigothic King Wamba. The work concludes with a scene of apotheosis depicting the House of Austria (Charles V, and the four Philips) as defenders of the faith. Cubillo turns to Josephus for the material in one of his most popular plays, *Los desagravios de Cristo* [The Vengeance of Christ],[29] one that depicts the destruction of Jerusalem in A.D. 70. The other two religious works are notably unremarkable attempts to deal with the genre of "saintly bandit" dramas.

The real importance of Cubillo de Aragón as a figure that will enable us to perceive the progress of the *comedia* in the period of 1631–1650 lies in the seven plays dealing with material original to him, as original that is as it was possible for him to be when dealing with the standard materials of the Spanish theater: the cape and sword play, palace plots, and the *figurón.* I have chosen two of these plays as examples of the developments most typical of Cubillo's best works.

El Señor de Buenas Noches [The Lord of Happy Nights].[30] This simply structured play, written in 1631 or 1632, approaches being a *comedia de figurón* but it cannot be so classified since the one of the two brothers who is depicted with the broad caricaturizing strokes typical of that subgenre, is not the protagonist of the play. Instead, the drama revolves around the character of his younger twin brother, who has inherited neither title nor wealth, and that of the lady who so arranges matters that she gets the husband of her choice. The Marquis Carlos is foolish, vain, envious, avaricious and stupid, and suffers from some nameless sexual disorder to boot. His brother Enrique is the true gallant, valiant and discreet hero of the Spanish *comedia,* one who is, in addition, dutifully respectful even toward his undeserving brother.

Act I. After an expository scene presented through the servants of the two brothers, the admirable twin Enrique agrees to leave his brother free from obligation to him if Carlos will speak on his behalf to Marcelo, Porcia's father, to arrange his marriage *(in).* Carlos, unreasoningly envious of his brother and wishing to deprive him of any happiness, asks for her hand for himself *(ra).* Porcia, when she learns that her father has agreed to the marriage, sends word to Carlos that she would like to talk to him at her window that evening *(ra).* Enrique appears there and is overwhelmed when the lady, believing him to be his brother, talks to him of marriage. She, in turn, is enchanted with the suitor *(ra).* When she complains to "Carlos" of his younger brother's past attentions, Enrique realizes the error; she does not *(ra).* Carlos appears on the scene and Enrique protects his position making Carlos retreat in cowardly fashion. Porcia believes that her suitor "Carlos" has bravely driven "Enrique" off *(ra).*

Act II. Unaware that the gentleman with whom she has fallen in love is Enrique, Porcia claims to have fallen for Carlos whom she defends against all who would remind her of his reputation, a reputation that she finds unwarranted *(ra).* Enrique, disillusioned by her acceptance of his brother, comes to take leave of his future sister-in-law as he gets ready to leave for Flanders. She is taken by his manner but still believes that Carlos is her man *(ra).* Her love, however, turns to worry when Carlos comes to visit and she finds that he is every bit the fool his reputation has made him to be *(pp).* Porcia accidentally overhears a conversation between the brothers that clarifies what happened as well as the fact that Carlos does not love her at all but only wants to take her from his brother *(pt).* She then begs Enrique's forgiveness, confesses her love for him, and asks him to stay. After making a show of leaving for the war front, Enrique goes into hiding at the house of a friend, suitor to Porcia's cousin, Dorotea *(rt).*

Act III. Enrique comes to Porcia to talk with her about their problem, but he must hide when her father enters to press for an immediate marriage *(pt).* By innuendo, Porcia and her maid Aldonza, convince Marcelo that, because Carlos seems to be suffering from some sexual incapacity, the wedding should be delayed *(rt).* When Carlos comes to press for an immediate wedding, his foolishness seems to confirm the suspicions about his sexual deviance and Marcelo tells Porcia to delay as she sees fit. Porcia does so by insisting that the wedding must await the arrival of her cousin, Enrique del Rincón (Henry from the Corner), who has been named "Lord of Happy Nights" *(pt)*. Ironically, Enrique is hiding at that very moment "in the corner." That evening when Enrique is again coming to Porcia's house to spend a "Happy Night" with her, he is surprised at the door by Carlos. His servant identifies him as Enrique del Rincón who has come to visit *(rt)*. Carlos then calls upon Porcia's father and asks to meet the cousin. Marcelo, aware that no such person exists, is shocked to hear that he is already in Porcia's room with her *(pt)*. The two go there to verify the presence of a male visitor *(ec)*. When Enrique identifies himself, Carlos is finally forced to acknowledge his brother's prior claim and the couple are married *(dt)*.

Particularly noticeable in dealing with this *comedia* is the extremely simple structure employed in it. No extraneous material of any kind, no subplot, distracts from the main thread of the story; yet the play falls short of the best that the Spanish Golden Age drama has to offer. This is due, in part, to the fact that Carlos, the older brother, falls short of being a true comic *figurón* because his actions with regard to Enrique are as malicious as his love-making is comic. Both as a character and as a caricature he is too contradictory. The audience cannot give itself over completely either to laugh at or to scorn him. The play also fails, in part, because Enrique is drawn as a character who is too perfect, too respectful toward his malevolent brother, too self-abnegating when it comes to his love for Porcia. The play, however, does have elements that lift it above the level of melodrama. Porcia is an intelligent, real human being, a woman who—in seventeenth-century Spain—reminds her father that she is a real person, that she is the one who is to be married, and that her acceptance of the marriage is a necessary element of it (156b). Undoubtedly, Cubillo himself felt some of the weaknesses present in this work because he later redeveloped some of the same materials into a full-fledged *comedia de figurón* in his *El invisible príncipe del baúl* [The Invisible Prince of Baúl],[31] which depends upon the *figurón*'s belief that he is invisible as long as he is wearing a certain feathered cap.

La perfecta casada [The Perfect Wife].³² a play that was performed before King Philip IV in December 1636, is a notable example of Cubillo's ability to combine simplicity of plot, characterization, and—probably—materials reflecting his knowledge of the works of earlier writers including dramatists.

Act I. Aurelio is faced with the dilemma over which of two relatives, suitors for his daughter Estefanía, is more worthy of her hand *(ex)*. He asks the King to decide *(in)*. When the general César returns victorious from a battle against the Turks, the King marries him to Estefanía instead of either of the two earlier suitors *(ra)*. César, however, is in love with Rosimunda, a beautiful captive he has brought back with him *(ex)*. In spite of the fact that this is clear to her, Estefanía unselfishly welcomes Rosimunda as a friend *(ra)*.

Act II. Dorotea, Estefanía's made, counterfeits and delivers identical love notes to the former suitors. Federico, the better of the two, destroys the note he does not intend to answer. Alejandro, the other, decides instead to come to Estefanía's aid *(ra)*. César, indifferent to the charms of his wife, spends his nights on the town. She willingly provides him with money so that he can do so in style *(ra)*. The King, aware of César's behavior, comes to see if he can help Estefanía but she sends him away claiming that she is the luckiest of wives and has the best of husbands *(pp)*. César, rather than gambling, spends a great deal of his time pursuing Rosimunda, who, even though she feels a mutual attraction, carefully guards her honor *(pt)*. When Alejandro comes to Estefanía's balcony, the King draws his sword to chase him away. César comes and joins in but then, not recognizing the King, demands to know his identity. When he draws his sword to attack, Estefanía comes out of the house, sword in hand, to join her husband in defense of her own honor and his *(rt)*.

Act III. The King will not grant César permission to return to the war until he is satisfied with regard to the marriage with Estefanía that he had arranged *(pt)*. The former suitors come calling on Estefanía who will not listen to any complaints against or gossip about her husband *(rt)*. First Rosimunda and then César come and hide on either side of the stage in order to eavesdrop on Estefanía *(pt)*. When she threatens her maid Dorotea with a dagger demanding to know what had been done to bring the former suitors into her house, they both admire the intelligence and wisdom that Estefanía uses in dealing with the problem *(rt)*. Estefanía then orders the male servant Calvatrueno to deliver a necklace of hers as a present to Rosimunda since the gold broach that César had ordered him to take to Rosimunda was too poor a gift; she goes to get the jewelry *(pt)*. Rosimunda and César both come out of hiding. Each has decided to respect the marriage and they tell each other so *(rt)*. When Estefanía returns with the necklace, she and César are reconciled and the King comes in to announce that Rosimunda is really César's sister who had been captured as a baby by the enemy Turks *(ec)*. Rosimunda and Federico are married as are Calvatrueno and Dorotea *(dt)*.

Not only does the play make use of well-worn motifs such as the long-lost child or sibling and the beautiful captive who is the object of a victorious general's love (see for example Mira de Amescua's *Wheel of Fortune* discussed earlier in Chapter 1), but he also employs not so common elements. Here, the unselfish, dutiful wife (taken of course in great part from Fray Luis de León's book *La perfecta casada*) who, after her guilty but penitent husband begs forgiveness, becomes reconciled to him seems to be closely related (because of parallel passages) to Mira's play *Gambler's Home*. Even more noticeable is the relationship of the work to its contemporary *The Husband Makes the Wife* (see above). Here the message is the mirror image of the thesis presented by Mendoza: "The wife makes the husband." Too often to have been accidental, phrases, verses, and *sententiae* have been lifted from Mendoza's play and used in a reversed manner. For example, Mendoza's "He who loves more, deserves more," appears here as "They who know how to love less, always deserve more" (118b).

We must conclude, then, that almost all of Cubillo de Aragón's plays, including the reworked historical plays and the religious pageants as well as the novelistic dramas, were artfully prepared rehashes and re-mixes of earlier materials. As such his work is representative of much of the theater written in the years between 1630 and 1650 whether by the "minor" dramatists or by the "major" figures. Many of Calderón's plays are reworkings to some extent. His *Los cabellos de Absalón* [Absalom's Hair], to cite only one example, incorporates verbatim an entire act from Tirso de Molina's *La venganza de Tamar* [Tamar's Vengeance]. The list of such rewritings, some of which were done for the purpose of setting pieces into a different aesthetic framework, others of which were prepared for simple commercial reasons, is endless. The practice became increasingly common as the genre aged. Cubillo was just as successful, if not more so, than most who worked in this fashion.

The developments of the period 1631–1650, one that we can recognize as centering around the theater of Pedro Calderón de la Barca, are ones in which the *comedias* as a whole demonstrate certain distinctive qualities: (1) The plot and subplot materials are so closely related that it is often difficult to distinguish them as separate entities. (2) The plot structure as a whole is simpler, less complicated, with fewer distracting elements, and is more unified. (3) This relative simplicity of plot and the consequent ease with which the action is portrayed brings with it a correlative element of longer yet more rhetorically dynamic speeches. (4) The plays are built as much around the characterizations presented as about the dramatic actions through which the characters are developed. (5) The authors who best typify the work of this period quite consciously sought new paths to follow such as the open use of the fact that the author, the actors, and the audience were all quite aware of the theatrical nature of what was going on. (6) Too, the dramatists made strong, conscious efforts to avoid trite conclusions for the commonplace situations around which the *comedias* were developed. (7) The more serious, at times didactic, intent of the best plays becomes obvious as the genre moved toward what might be called social comedy. (8) The increasing poetic sophistication of the ordinary theatergoing public, an audience grown accustomed to verbal and theatrical conventions through prolonged contact with the theater, is obviously demonstrated by the increased use of highly stylized Baroque language and rhetoric.

The reasons for these developments lay in part in the changing political and literary situations as well as in actual changes in the theaters and stages where the works were presented.

Chapter Five
The Post-Calderonian Dramatists (1651–1700)

The last fifty years of the seventeenth century are years that in general saw a remarkable increase in the number of writers trying their hand at the writing of *comedias,* with a consequent general decrease in the individuality of efforts and in the quality of results. I have previously shown how changes in the personal situation of Pedro Calderón de la Barca brought on a real decrease in his dramatic productivity after 1651. The reopening of the court and public theaters that same year brought with it an increased demand for new dramatic texts, a demand that was soon filled by a host of lesser dramatists who hastened to fill the gap. They did so, in many cases, by resorting to the practice of reworking earlier plays in such a way as to fit them more closely to aesthetic principles then in vogue, to the stricter censorship being enforced by the Inquisition, or to the demands of public taste.

In reworking earlier pieces, or even in writing completely new works, poets held rather strictly to the principles of structure and the themes that had already proved to be successful: the honor drama, the cape and sword comedy, and the historical plays. Two currents, with roots based in earlier periods, soon developed into the *comedia* types into which the greatest amounts of individuality and inventiveness were to be poured: the full-fledged *comedia de figurón* and the mythological drama.

Both of these fit particularly well into the changing artistic mold of the time. The *comedia de figurón* as a genre was easily used for demonstrating various foolishness and foibles of the human kind. The mythological play lent itself easily to the increasingly visual and aural nature of the theater. Some pieces of this type became true *zarzuelas* (operettas) with the consequent mixture of poetry, drama, music, dance, and scenic art. Fortunately, a good part of one such production,

Juan (1611–1675, the son of Luis) Vélez de Guevara's *Los celos hacen estrellas* [Jealousy Makes Stars], remains.[1] Besides the text, we have a good portion of the music and some watercolor drawings of the set designs used in its presentation.

One playwright alone among the major figures of the seventeenth century wrote most of his *comedias* (some fifty-two plays) during the latter half of that period. The dramatic art of Agustín Moreto, who, besides creating works uniquely his own, rewrote a number of earlier plays to bring them into tune with the times, has been studied by both Ruth Lee Kennedy and Frank P. Casa.[2] A review of their conclusions shows that his work falls well within the model here proposed as typical of the late *comedia*.

The fact is that between the first decades and the last half of the seventeenth century there had been basic changes in the aesthetic principles that informed the *comedia*. Whereas, in the earliest period, the *comedia* was an open, vital, developing genre for which structures and guiding principles were yet being formulated; in the last years of the century both the format and the moral-aesthetic foundation had become regulated, set formations.

When Lope de Vega wrote his *New Art of Writing Plays* in 1609, he not only detailed the thematic, structural, and poetic practices he followed at the time, he also forthrightly proclaimed the justice of including in his plays materials that would appeal to the lower tastes of the common herd since, after all, they supported the theaters financially and thus they provided the market for his *comedias*.[3] The extent to which the writers of the Lopean period followed this precept is only too evident in the plays by Miguel Sánchez, Felipe Godínez, Diego Jiménez de Enciso, and Luis de Belmonte Bermúdez as reported earlier here.

By the end of the century, preceptists were describing contemporary dramatic practice in quite different terms. The proof that the practices they described were actually being practiced is probably best exemplified by the emphasis placed on the principle of *decorum* in the works. For Lope and those of his period this meant that the tone and vocabulary of each character's speeches should match that character's social position.[4] For the later writers, the principle involved became one of good taste. Francisco de Bances Candamo (a dramatist whose plays are to be studied below) was, as Moir and Wilson claim, "The only playwright of the Calderonian school who attempted to write an *Ars poetica.*"[5] In it he explicated the principles of dramatic practice and taste followed by writers of his period. In the version of his *Teatro de los teatros* [Theater of Theaters][6] written in 1689 and 1690, he reviews the history of the Spanish drama condemning the crudity and lack of decorum he finds in the early Lopean theater and giving a clear description of his own conception of decorum and of poetic, as opposed to historic, truth. In his discussion, for example, of Antonio Coello's *El conde de Sex* [The Count of Essex], he defends Coello's light-handed treatment of the blameworthy Queen Elizabeth I of England by claiming:

> It is an inviolable rule of the *comedia* that none of the characters should perform a shameful act, nor should they commit any low folly or indecent thing. Since, how can a Princess be presented in an unworthy fashion? Even more so when poetry is used to correct history, because the latter presents things as they are, but the former puts them as they should be (35).

The importance of these matters lies not just in helping to define the changes in artistic sensibilities that were taking place in the seventeenth century but in the fact that they show the Spanish theater moving independently toward Neoclassic norms under its own power, unaffected as yet by the influences from France to which that movement has generally been traced. Just as the French dramatists of the middle and late seventeenth and early eighteenth centuries (Corneille, Molière, Racine, Rotrou, etc.) went about bringing plays based on or translated from Spanish models into line with their own aesthetic ideas by unifying the dramatic structures, ridding the plots of distracting elements, and eliminating scenes they considered to be in bad taste (witness Corneille's cutting, in *Le Cid,* of Rodrigo's sharing his plate with a leper as in his model, Guillén de Castro's *Las mocedades del Cid),* the Spanish dramatists of the same period spent great effort in performing similar operations as they reworked earlier plays. The Spanish writers even used the newer norms, increasingly as the century moved on, when preparing new materials for the stage. The acceptance of this model for aesthetic movement in the Spanish *comedia,* a model that deserves much more thorough study than can be given it here, brings with it the corollary acceptance of a view of the movement of Spanish drama into the Neoclassic style as an evolutionary change rather than the abrupt departure from Golden Age practice that is generally described by literary historians.

As the number of *comedias* increased, the average number of plays each composed decreased. Many can hardly be described as playwrights since we have only one, two, or three texts that can be used to judge their work. Typically, too, these later dramatists were members of the court who wrote as a pleasant pastime or as a way to seek royal favor. Therefore, it was only natural that they should seek to follow the *comedia* recipe rather than to concoct entirely new combinations. Thus, their work suffers from the restraints imposed by the rules and artistic mood of the time. The creativity of these relatively inexperienced writers tended to be muffled, if not completely stifled, by their attempts to match their work to the rules rather than to allow the formulae to grow from the work as did Lope de Vega. Still, from among the fifty or so known dramatists of the period, I have had to choose three who, to me, best demonstrate the various facets of this stage in the life of the *comedia* in an inventive, individual fashion: Agustín de Salazar y Torres, Sor Juana Inés de la Cruz, and Francisco Antonio de Bances y López-Candamo.

There were many others among the group of late seventeenth-century writers whose work might have been chosen just as well: (1) Antonio de Solís y Ribadeneyra (1610–1686), like most a part-time playwright and member of the court, wrote some plays and reworkings of others in collaboration as well as some twelve *comedias* of his own. He developed a set pattern for the love intrigues in the cape and sword plays that has been commented on by Eduardo Juliá Martínez.[7] (2) Juan de Matos Fragoso (1610?–1692) wrote several plays of dramatic interest, but his best work is undoubtedly the reworking of Lope de Vega's *El villano en su rincón* [The Farmer in His Own Corner].[8] (3) Jerónimo de Cuéllar y La Chaux (1622–after 1665), another courtier, wrote, among other things, an interesting historical drama based on the trial of Gabriel de Espinosa that took place after the disappearance of Portugal's King Sebastián, *El pastelero de Madrigal* [The Pastry Cook from Madrigal].[9] (4) Juan de la Hoz y Mota (1622–1714) has left us at least a dozen *comedia* texts of which the best is his *El castigo de la miseria* [The

Punishment of Poverty], in which he combines a highly comic *figurón* of the same type as used by Molière in *L'Avare* with the story line of a tale written by María de Zayas, who gave it the same title.[10]

(5) Juan Bautista Diamante (1625–1687), another courtier, wrote a few texts of his own. Among others his *La reina María Estuarda* [The Queen Mary Stuart] and his *La magdalena de Roma* [The Magdalene of Rome], which treats the conversion of a courtesan, merit further study. Other than these, most of the texts we have from his hand are reworkings, more or less successful, of earlier plays.[11] (6) Francisco de Leiva Ramírez de Arellano (1630–1676) wrote plays from Roman history, some cape and sword dramas, at least one *comedia de figurón,* and the interesting *La dama presidente* [Lady President], in which the ladies take on male roles.[12] (7) Antonio de Zamora (1660?–1728), also a member of the Spanish court and part-time dramatist, is best remembered for two of his own creations that stand out from among the more than two dozen plays attributed to him: *La doncella de Orleáns* [The Maid of Orleáns], one of the first plays to deal with Joan of Arc, and *El hechizado por fuerza* [Bewitched by Force], one of the very best and most hilarious of the *comedias de figurón.* Although these two are probably his most important contributions to the Spanish stage, he is best known for his reworking of Tirso de Molina's *El burlador de Sevilla* [Trickster from Seville], the first of the Don Juan plays. This reworking as *El convidado de piedra* [The Stone Guest] is the form of the play that was responsible more than any other for the popular acceptance of the theme. Certainly it was Zamora's work that first spread, via translation, to the rest of Europe.[13]

Besides those named, all of whom deserve much more attention than I am free to give them here, there are more than forty lesser-known dramatists whose work we can identify and a host of anonymous writers who prepared *comedias* in the last half of the seventeenth century. The field of possible investigation seems endless. Perhaps new clues to help us comprehend the history of Spanish dramatic art lie still hidden among those works I have not had time to examine; however, I have chosen three writers who seem to me (at the present time) to be representative of the best the period has to offer.

Agustín de Salazar y Torres (1642–1675)

Born in Almazán, only a few years before Tirso de Molina's death there, Salazar y Torres traveled to Mexico as a child. He studied there, distinguishing himself at the university in the fields of law and theology. He returned to Spain with the Duke of Albuquerque and served with him in both German and Sicilian campaigns. He died at the age of thirty-three in Madrid. His friend Juan de Vera Tassis y Villarroel, who later published the theater of Calderón, published two volumes of Salazar y Torres's literary works as *La cítara de Apolo* [Apollo's Zither] in 1681 and 1694. The first volume contains only one play, the second is devoted to the rest of his theatrical works. The greater part of his drama is devoted to the mythological plays or spectacles that were so popular at court such as his *Eurídice y Orfeo, Thetis y Peleo,* and *Los juegos olímpicos* [The Olympic Games]; however, I have chosen to discuss here the two most accessible and perhaps the best dramas he wrote in his short life: *El encanto es la hermosura* [The Enchantment Is Beauty], also known as *La segunda Celestina* [The Second Celestine], and his *Elegir al enemigo* [To Choose the Enemy].[14]

To Choose the Enemy.[15]   This *comedia* is a real mixture of types familiar, by this time, to all. A cape and sword drama that takes place in a mythological time and place, it is set against the background of a fictional war between the island kingdoms of Cyprus and Crete. The poet makes full use of the setting to add verisimilitude of an ironic nature to the imagery he employs in the highly stylized verse so typical of the later *comedias*. Yet he manages, in spite of the rhetorical nature of the verse he writes, to get the play off to a fast, rousing start. A pair of shipwrecked men appear on stage (an interest-catching device in that period when coastal wrecks were much more common than in modern times),[16] and after an extremely economical sixty-five verses of expository material, an even more exciting initiating action takes place.

Act I. In a storm, Aristeo, the Prince of Cyprus, has lost not only his fleet but his beloved Nise, whom he was unwillingly escorting, en route, to an arranged marriage in Rhodes. He and his servant, the *gracioso* Escaparate, have been washed ashore on the enemy island of

Crete. They hear a song in which the lover is enjoined to choose between fire and water just as simultaneous appeals for help come from two directions: one lady is aboard a skiff being wrecked on nearby shoals, the other seeks escape from the flames approaching her rooms. He goes to rescue the latter *(in)*. He returns with the swooning Rosimunda, Princess of Crete, in his arms. Certain that Nise had perished in the ship wreck, Aristeo has fallen in love with Rosimunda *(ra)*. The King of Crete enters along with Ricardo, one of two official suitors for the hand of Rosimunda, and under his urging, the King has Aristeo imprisoned as the probable arsonist *(ra)*. Astolfo, the second official suitor of Rosimunda enters carrying the unconscious Nise whom he has rescued from the waters that were engulfing her boat. He has fallen in love with her *(ra)*. Nise recovers, tells her story, and agrees to remain in the palace as companion to Rosimunda *(ra)*. Ricardo, the real arsonist, has secretly freed Aristeo from prison and has hidden him in a tunnel leading to Rosimunda's chambers. There Aristeo and Nise face each other and it becomes clear that she still loves him but that her love is now unreciprocated *(ra)*.

Act II. Rosimunda and Nise trade confidences to the accompaniment of a song to which they in turn join their voices *(ra)*. The music continues as Astolfo and Ricardo enter to sing of their love by glossing the song being sung *(ra)*. The King enters, announces the innocence of the imprisoned Aristeo, and asks the two suitors to join him in a search for the real arsonist *(ra)*. When Aristeo enters, Nise identifies him as the Cypriot courtier "Fisberto," an identification he accepts in view of the personal danger the truth would cause *(ra)*. He, in turn, openly declares his love to Rosimunda, a declaration she allows him to make without interruption *(pp)*. That evening Rosimunda goes to the garden to dream of her love for "Fisberto" and is sleeping there when he comes in response to a request from Nise *(rt)*. He is followed by Astolfo and Ricardo who have each suborned one of Rosimunda's ladies-in-waiting to allow them access to the garden. In the dark, Aristeo confuses Nise with Rosimunda and declares his love for the latter *(pt)*. Angry, Nise calls for help and to their own great confusion, the various principals come out all at once. They agree to avoid scandal by each leaving the garden to go his own way *(rt)*.

Act III. Ricardo comes to seek Aristeo's (Fisberto's) help in resolving the dispute with Astolfo over the hand of Rosimunda. In the process, Aristeo's confidence in Rosimunda's love for him is badly shaken *(pt)*. He and Rosimunda then share a musical scene in which she again gives him hope *(rt)*. Nise enters to tell Rosimunda that her father wants to see her. Then Nise and Aristeo share a musical scene that causes the eavesdropping Rosimunda to mistrust the love of Aristeo *(pt)*. The King announces that Rosimunda is to decide at once which of her suitors she will accept *(rt)*. The entire court convenes, and to the accompaniment of song, Rosimunda is about to choose when the news of the arrival of the Cypriot fleet interrupts the proceedings. The Prince is, at last, identified and Rosimunda, with a vacillation that increases the dramatic tension, finally announces that Aristeo is her choice for a husband *(ec)*. He agrees, Astolfo is married to Nise, Ricardo to one of the other Cypriot princesses, and Escaparate is refused by the maid Estela, all to the accompaniment of the same song that forms the background for the last half of this third act *(dt)*.

The most notable difference between this *comedia* and others is certainly the use made of songs and music. Earlier *comedias* also used occasional songs to a greater or lesser extent, some even with structural intent, as has been shown in studies made of the songs used in *comedias* by Lope de Vega, Tirso de Molina, and Calderón de la Barca.[17] But in this *comedia* the songs come to be something other than incidental: (1) songs are used to underscore both the initiating incident and the emotional climax; (2) several of the songs are sung by the principal characters, rather than by offstage musicians; and (3) the third act is completely informed by the music of three songs. If the work had any but the standard three-act format and typical *comedia* structure it would better be classed as a musical piece rather than drama. An example of the extent to which the music was used is best noted in the stage directions found in the third act to introduce the musical scene between Nise and Aristeo: "From this verse on, without stopping the dramatic action, the following verse is to be sung" (280c). Even more revealing is another stage direction in which the timing of the action is tied to the accompanying music: "The lines that follow are to be acted in the time that the music lasts" (281c). There can be no doubt that this work represents some sort of intermediate step in the history of the theater.

Several other facets of the work also merit mention. As has been noted before, the Spanish *comedia* could often demonstrate a self-conscious awareness of its own theatricality. This is shown here by such lines as those that close *Act I:*

ESCAPARATE: Let's leave, Sir; By God,
this palace is enchanted
according to the spot I'm in,
even if it is a play's predicament.   (271a)

Another aspect of earlier *comedia* structure that is present here is the constant mirroring of the principal actions by the lower social types (the *gracioso* and maids) as a source of humor of ironic or satiric nature. Still another element is the use of well-known literature as a source for commentary of one kind or another. For example, in the third act Escaparate several times quotes from a very well-known love sonnet by Garcilaso de la Vega (1501–1536).[18]

Not so frequently seen in other plays is the care taken here to maintain a unity of atmosphere. All the characters react quite regularly, as would people of the mythological place and time where the story takes place. Only the *gracioso* is allowed to separate himself from the past. What anachronisms (a common fault of the early *comedia*) do exist seem to fall deliberately from the lips of Escaparate. When he and Aristeo first hear music, the *gracioso* proclaims it to be some sacristan practicing his "Kyries."

In conclusion, *To Choose the Enemy* is an excellent representative of the final stage in the development of the *comedia,* one well worth further study. The same may be claimed for the second work by Salazar y Torres that is to be studied here, *El encanto es la hermosura* [The Enchantment is Beauty].

The Enchantment is Beauty.[19]   This play, according to its first editor, Juan de Vera Tassis, was left unfinished on his death by Salazar y Torres, who had planned the piece for the birthday celebration of Queen Mariana de Austria. He had written the first two acts and a good piece of the third. Vera Tassis claims to have finished the work upon royal request.[20] The play is constructed around a standard love intrigue presented, although with some freshness of approach, in the usual *comedia* format, into which characters taken from Fernando de Rojas's *Celestina* (1499) are closely interwoven.

Act I. The play begins with ear and eye-catching abruptness when Doña Beatriz, on her way to visit her cousin Doña Ana in Seville, comes onto the scene in hunting costume and with a gun. She threatens Don Juan who, taken by her beauty, has been following her *(in)*. Juan remains behind as she leaves. He is found by his two servants, the *gracioso* Tacón and the roguish Muñoz. Their conversation gives the needed information about the situation. Juan is returning to Seville because of family responsibilities there. He had left for Flanders after wounding a man he had found talking at the balcony of Ana. He is sure that she had betrayed him *(ex)*. Muñoz informs Juan that he knows the wily daughter of Celestina who should be able to help him locate and identify the beautiful huntress. Tacón, fearful of Celestina's witchcraft (a skill that Muñoz denies to her), warns against using her *(ra)*. Antonia, servant to Ana, comes to ask Celestina to find out, for her mistress, whether or not she will ever see her beloved Juan again *(ra)*. Through a bit of perspectivistic exposition we find out that the gentleman Juan had wounded was Don Diego, an unrequited suitor who had approached Ana's balcony with the help of Antonia and Celestina. After being paid, Celestina agrees to help Ana in this. Then Juan comes to seek her help in the matter of the mysterious huntress. First, gaining his confidence by displaying her unaccounted-for knowledge of past events, Celestina agrees, upon being paid, to help in this, too. She asks him to meet her at the house of Don Luis, Ana's father, after she has had time to verify the facts. He, since he has brought Luis letters from Flanders, agrees *(ra)*. On his way, Juan runs into Diego who is being attacked by several men and comes to his rescue since he does not know the identity of his rival *(ra)*. Celestina tells Ana that she will soon see Juan. Then Juan calls at the door. Ana is frightened by what appears to her to be witchcraft. Juan believes her fright to be due to her unfaithfulness *(ra)*. When Ana at last runs off, Juan faces Celestina only to be surprised by the sudden appearance of Beatriz. His disbelief in witchcraft is shaken to the core *(ra)*.

Act II. Luis, anxious to identify the man who has been hanging around, informs his daughter Ana that he is leaving but will return soon *(ra)*. The maid Antonia, at Celestina's urging, plans to let Diego into the house so that he can approach Ana *(ra)*. Beatriz confides in Ana about her love for Diego, whose whereabouts she does not know. Ana promises to get Celestina to help her *(ra)*. Juan enters and places Ana on the defensive since he had reason (a strange man at her balcony) to doubt her faithfulness. She becomes angry, at which point Beatriz enters, recognizes Juan as the man who had been after her in the forest, and tells Ana of the incident. This puts Juan, then, on the defensive *(pp)*. At this point Celestina returns, followed closely by Luis.

Celestina takes advantage of the confused situation to impute thievery to Tacón and heroism to Juan. Luis throws Tacón out of the house after making him return "Celestina's" jewel, and welcomes Juan to his house *(rt)*. In a scene reflecting what had earlier happened between Celestina and Ana, Beatriz seeks help in locating Diego who, as if by magic, appears. Diego tries to convince Beatriz of his love for her, but when Ana enters, he turns to attempt to convince them of his simultaneous love for both *(pt)*. As Luis and Celestina are about to enter, the ladies hide Diego in an adjoining chamber and ask Celestina's help in getting him safely and secretly out of the house *(rt)*. She, when forced by Luis to reveal the identity of the unknown suitor, takes advantage of the situation and a handy mirror, to conjure up the vision of Diego in the mirror as he leaves behind the entranced Luis *(pt)*.

Act III. Luis goes to Celestina for more help in identifying the suspicious suitor, but a knock at the door sends him into hiding. As she answers the door, Celestina remarks that this is the first *comedia* in which the old man has had to hide. Tacón has come to reclaim the jewel she had tricked him out of, but Celestina "conjures up" Luis, and Tacón is forced to "return" to Celestina his pouch of coins. Celestina then tells Luis the name of the man he saw in the mirror, Diego *(rt)*. [21] Ana and Beatriz are discussing the foibles of the two gentlemen when Celestina comes with the news that Luis is about to force Diego into a marriage with Ana *(pt)*. Ana's only hope is to get Juan to come. Celestina uses the mirror to bring him in for an interview. After declaring her love, Ana faints. He hides, eavesdropping as Beatriz comes to help Ana. Celestina then pulls the same trick on Beatriz but, rather than faint, she walks out just as Luis enters and Diego must hide *(rt)*. Celestina then tells Luis that she had been in error before but will now show him the true lovers, in turn. She makes use of the mirror again as the two young men go off to an appointed duel *(pt)*. Celestina sends Luis after them. The law called by Tacón is after Celestina but first runs into the men. To ensure that no duel will take place they follow them all back home. They find Celestina there, but one at a time she explains away the charges of witchcraft, finally admitting the presence of the young men in the house and the use of the mirror. Luis draws his sword intent on his honor *(ec)*, but is pacified when Juan agrees to marry Ana, and Diego takes Beatriz. The two pairs of servants match off as well *(dt)*.

The *Enchantment Is Beauty* is a good example of a play in which the overcharged rhetoric of the Baroque is used with good effect to embroider beautiful designs about the stuff from which *comedias* were made, to supply audial and intellectual interest if the action failed. These flights of verbal fancy seem, however, to require that the underlying structures of the piece be simple in order to stabilize the results. Here a well-known comic situation (two pairs of lovers, parted by misunderstanding and coincidence) is interwoven carefully with elements from one of the best known stories from early Spanish fiction in a symmetrical, constantly self-reinforcing fashion. The faithfulness with which the poets retain the character of Celestina is remarkable. She is her old, wily, opportunistic self, well known to all who deal with her, and as avaricious as always. The two servants Tacón and Muñoz even react to her in the same ways as do those in Rojas's novel. The difference here is that this is one of Celestina's flings with love that works, one that is comic rather than tragic. Granted that Juan de Vera Tassis did indeed complete the work that Salazar y Torres began, the great unity of plot and style indicate several things. First, Salazar must have left not only the text of the two first acts and a good bit of the third, but he must have left as well some sort of sketch for the completed work. Vera Tassis did not find it necessary to add one bit of expository material for his conclusion. This indicates either a highly stylized method of plot construction or that a carefully prepared sketch had been prepared. I would tend to believe that both possibilities were at work here. Second, the unity of style between the two poets is highly unusual if not unique. The same two sets of possibilities exist to explain this circumstance and I would draw the same conclusion with regard to the style.

The work is clearly theatrical and self-consciously so. If the speeches cited above in which the characters talk about the work itself are not sufficient proof, Celestina's remarks and actions in the final scene certainly are. She says, in an aside to the audience, that "They say that a play lasts as long as its plot" (264a). She then goes on in what would, in musical terms, be called a false cadence to trick Tacón into agreeing to marry her. He does so but claims that he can prove force (thus gaining ground for annulment). She then demurs on the grounds that he had previously promised marriage to the maid Antonia. At this Tacón calls on the audience to witness the fact that, in the entire play, he has not spoken one word to Antonia. Celestina's reply, one that finally forces him to agree, is that "In secret, between the acts, you did make love to her" (264c). The metatheatrical process was certainly in full swing!

Sor Juana Inés de la Cruz (1651–1695)

Born Juana Inés de Asbaje y Ramírez de Cantillana in Mexico, the future nun of great literary talent was certainly one of the world's prodigies. For biographical detail and for commentary on her nontheatrical works, I refer those interested to the volume in this same series dedicated to her. [22] It has been generally assumed that, as a colonial writer, Sor Juana was somewhat belated in her following of literary trends coming from the peninsula and she is, therefore, commonly written of as an anachronistic member of the Calderonian school. I hope that this study will show that such is not the case. Her plays show exactly the same tendencies and developments as found in the works of her post-Calderonian contemporaries. Besides the four *autos sacramentales* that fall outside our field of interest here, Sor Juana wrote two true *comedias* (or at least one and two-thirds *comedias* if contrary claims to the authorship of the second act of one of them are accepted): *Los empeños de una casa* [The Desires of One House] and *El amor es más laberinto* [Love is the Greater Labyrinth].

The Desires of One House. [23]   As if she intuitively recognized the need for extreme simplicity and symmetry in the structure of the play as a means for keeping the audience from becoming lost in the manneristic jungle of events and rhetoric that forms the text, Sor Juana underscores with action and attention grabbing poetry the key structural points in her drama. Once these points are set, we can easily recognize the way in which each action leading up to the pivotal point at the center is mirrored in the events that follow, thus forming a simple, stable, and symmetrically modeled whole.

Act I. The six main events of the first act (numbered for convenience in the order of their occurence) that are reflected by those of the third act are as follows: (1) Doña Ana, speaking with her servant while awaiting the arrival of Leonor, the beloved of her brother, Don Pedro, tells how he had planned to kidnap Leonor after hearing how she has planned to elope with Don Carlos before her father can force her to accept another suitor. In ignorance of the love between Carlos and Leonor, and disregarding her own former feelings for Don Juan, Ana has fallen in love with Carlos herself *(ex)*. (2) The kidnapped Leonor is left at the house, in Ana's care, by certain "constables" while still others carry Carlos away as a prisoner. Leonor is taken to Ana's room as Carlos, having escaped, seeks refuge coincidentally in the same house. Taking advantage of the situation to tie Carlos to herself by bonds of obligation, Ana hides him in another room *(in)*. (3) Meanwhile Rodrigo, Leonor's father, hears of her elopement but believes her to have left with her most stubborn suitor Pedro. He decides to approach Pedro immediately to demand marriage *(ra)*. (4) In Ana's darkened room, Juan, having bribed her servant to gain entry, attempts to rape Leonor, believing her to be Ana. Leonor screams and both Ana and Carlos come. In the dark Carlos and Leonor seem about to get together, as do Juan and Ana, and all seems about to be resolved when the servant Celia brings in lights *(ra)*. (5) The light brings utter confusion since no one understands or can explain the presence of others there. Leonor suspects the loyalty of Carlos. He distrusts the motives of Juan. Juan doubts the love of Ana. And she cannot understand how Juan came to be in her room *(ra)*. (6) There is no time for any one to clear matters up since Pedro arrives on the scene and all are forced into hiding in separate rooms, of course, to protect the honor of Doña Ana. She greets her brother as if nothing had happened and the two plot some way to help him gain the acceptance of Leonor *(ra)*.

Act II. The second act centers on a lyric scene with two actions on each side of it (the numbering of the events continues as for act one): (7) Carlos plans, with his servant Castaño, several ways in which he might get both himself and Leonor out of the house *(ra)*. (8) A series of scenes that shows how Ana tries first to convince Leonor of Carlos's infidelity and then to convince him of Leonor's interest in Pedro *(ra)*. (9) In this central scene, a musical one, the characters, each in turn, gloss the song to present the status of their feelings. Carlos, it seems, is jealous but still certain of Leonor's love for him and his for her. He decides to rescue her by any means necessary *(pp)*. (From this point on, the numbering established for the first half of the play is used to indicate how the episodes of the second half are related to earlier events.) (8) Reflecting the action preceding the lyric central one, Rodrigo comes to the house and, while Carlos listens in, obtains Pedro's promise to marry Leonor if she is willing *(pt)*. (7) Castaño advises Carlos to avenge himself on Pedro by taking advantage of Ana's love for him, but he refuses, remaining firm in his love for Leonor *(rt)*.

Act III. The actions of the last act reflect those of the first, as the numbering indicates: (6) Everyone is in various rooms of the house. Celia has placed Carlos in one room, Leonor in another, and given Juan the key to the garden *(rt)*. (5) Castaño, dressed as a woman, runs into Pedro as he tries to escape. Pedro believing the "lady" to be Leonor asks her hand in marriage. Castaño promises to marry Pedro if he will accept the "lady" as she is. Great confusion erupts as Ana comes out trying to stop a fight between Carlos and Juan. With everyone on stage and chaos reigning, Castaño puts out the lights *(pt)*. (4) In the dark everything is rearranged and straightened out. Carlos runs into Leonor and, believing her to be Ana to whom he owes life and honor, he leads her from the house to escape her brother's ire. Ana runs into Juan and, believing him to be Carlos, leads him back to her own room and bed. Pedro, still believing Castaño to be Leonor, locks him into still another room and goes off in search of his sister *(rt)*. (3) Rodrigo sets off to ensure the marriage of Leonor to Pedro *(pt)*. (2) Carlos, unconsciously correcting his earlier crime, returns Leonor to the hands of her father in the belief that he is indeed giving him Ana to protect. The dramatic irony of this scene, as only the lady and the audience realize what is truly happening, is climactic *(ec)*. (1) In the last scenes all is clarified. Ana, having given herself to Juan, accepts him in marriage. Leonor, with the blessing of her father, marries Carlos. And Pedro, the would-be trickster, is fooled as his "lady" Castaño marries the maid Celia *(dt)*.

Sor Juana has poetically and structurally underscored her main theme by encrusting it in the central scene that is set apart by the use of music and poetry. In this scene the musicians ask, "Which is the greatest pain suffered by those in love?" (192c). The answer is provided by five stanzas of the song: the lack of response from the beloved, jealousy, impatience while waiting to consummate one's love, worry about losing one's love, or enforced continence. Each stanza ends with the refrain, "Yes it's so! No, it's not!" (292c). The song is then glossed by each of those present on stage. Each claims that the problem he is suffering from is the worst. Pedro complains about the lack of response from Leonor, Ana about the jealousy she feels toward Leonor on account of Carlos, Carlos about the worries he has because of Leonor and Juan, and finally Castaño and Celia air their complaints: he that he has nothing to give Celia and she that he has nothing with which to pay.

This scene occurs framed by the symmetrical structure of the second act, an act whose main purpose is to demonstrate the fidelity and love of Carlos for Leonor. At each side of the central scene are found various plots aimed against the love of Carlos and Leonor, but the first and last scenes of the act are used to emphasize his loyalty to her. Yet the basic symmetry of structure is not limited to the second act; it is reinforced by that of the first and the third acts. To demonstrate this we need only to cite, first, the scenes in which everyone is hidden in the house, an action that ends the first act and begins the last, and second, the two scenes in which Rodrigo seeks remedy for his wounded honor. Even more important, however, is the intrinsic symmetry of the main action, that is, the use of the *confusion-order* dichotomy that is so carefully linked to the *darkness-light* symbols in acts I and III.

In Act I, the four main characters are all in one dark room, each still sure of what he most wants. Juan wants to enjoy Ana's sexual favors and, in the belief that she has entered the room, he pursues Leonor. Ana desires to ensure the love of Carlos for her. Carlos, having sought refuge in order to be able later to get together with Leonor, answers screams for help. And Leonor, having been left in Ana's care, can only think of her separated Carlos. When light is brought onto the stage, all this certainty disappears and thus are taken the first steps toward the "pains of love" so lyrically treated in the second act. If this scene existed in a structural vacuum, we might remain unsure about the deliberate intention of the *dark-light* image. But in the third act, the same sort of action is found in reverse, bringing about the conclusion of the *comedia.* This repetition itself reinforces the importance and effect of the symbolization. Pedro is with Castaño (believing him to be Leonor) when Ana, Carlos, and Juan break onto the stage. All is confusion. Immediately Castaño puts out the light and the couples, in the dark, get together in the right order. In this scene, then, the darkness functions in such a way as to put an end to the preceding disorder. Thus we arrive at a comprehension of the auto-negative correspondence of *light* bringing *confusion* and *darkness* bringing *order,* another facet of the refrain from the central song "Yes it's so! No, it's not!"

Finally, I would cite the basic symmetry of the initiating action, that action that begins the intrigue, or rather that which disturbs the equilibrium of the theatrical world presented by Sor Juana, and the emotional climax or moment of greatest tension between what might happen and that which does occur, a tension that is resolved in the denouement. Here, certainly, the initiating action is Leonor's precipitous elopement leaving her father's house and her arrival at that of Ana. She has broken with the social norms of the time. The emotional climax of the work, put into dramatic relief by the irony of the situation, is the moment when Leonor is returned to her father's care by the same man with whom she had left. Social order is thus restored and the *comedia* can end happily.

Love Is the Greater Labyrinth. [24]   The symmetry noted in dealing with *The Desires of One House* might be accidental if it were not found in other plays of the time and, above all, in the second of Sor Juana's *comedias,* the title of which exposes the central theme. [25] In dealing with the theme of love as a labyrinth, the drama is constructed about the mythological tale of Theseus and the Minotaur, bringing it well into line with the principles of the cape and sword drama.

Just as in her other *comedia,* the central scene of this one is of lyric nature: a scene of singing and dancing at a masked ball in the palace. Each character, in turn, glosses the song applying it to his own case. The technique is even more finely developed here than in the earlier play. The four principals who will marry at the end (Theseus and Phaedra, Bacchus and Ariadne) gloss the song in the form of lyric *décimas* (a highly formalized ten-verse stanza); the four minor characters, Lidoro (a gallant who is killed), Laura, Atún, and Cintia (servants), also gloss the song but in *quintillas* (a less formal five-verse stanza). Thus the latter reflect and emphasize the central theme presented by the former. This type of mirroring action by servants, as we have seen, is quite typical of the *comedia.*

The entire second act is built around the masked ball during which the labyrinth of love achieves its greatest confusion. The action of the second act preceding the ball itself has to do with the signals sent by both Ariadne and Phaedra to Theseus asking that he wear them so that they can recognize him. Laura brings the ribbon from Phaedra. Cintia arrives with a feather from Ariadne. Theseus decides to wear the ribbon sending his servant Atún, dressed in high fashion, to wear the feather. This results in the series of events that create the labyrinth of love. Atún loses the feather, Bacchus picks it up, Ariadne makes a date with Bacchus, then, instead of Theseus. After the masked ball, in a dark room that is the place where the various couples had planned to meet, all four appear as does Lidoro, the third gallant. The act as a whole is set symmetrically by these actions, but one further symmetry must also be noted: The act begins with Theseus's exit from the real labyrinth and ends when he is forced to hide there again. The labyrinth then figures in the act both in literal as well as in figurative terms.

There is a symmetry of structure in the first and third acts as well. The initiating action is found in the arrival of Theseus at the court of Minos and the sacrifice that Minos orders there. The emotional climax is recognized in the death sentence ordered by the aggrieved King Minos for all, almost at the same moment when the Athenian army arrives to avenge the supposed death of their Prince Theseus. The second action of the first act is found in the way in which both Phaedra and Ariadne fall in love with Theseus even though both had previously been in love with Bacchus. This action is reflected in the third act when the two pairs of lovers make a frustrated attempt at an elopement (Ariadne with Bacchus in the belief that she is with Theseus). In the last scene of the first act, King Minos puts an end to a duel that has erupted between Bacchus and Lidoro because of jealousy over supposed favors each has received from the ladies. The third act begins with just a scene. Minos stops the duel to ask for Bacchus's help in the inevitable war with Athens.

Presented in this way, the structure of the *comedia* seems more simple than it is in truth. It only seems so because I have grouped minor actions and decorative scenes, and because I have eliminated almost all mention of the ever present mirroring actions. Nevertheless the scheme presented here is, I believe, accurate and faithful to the simplicity and symmetry at the base of the original work.

In conclusion, I believe that Sor Juana was quite aware of what she was doing as she structured her plays in this fashion. Such structures do not occur by accident. She knew how to apply the resources she had at hand (dance, music, and verse) in order to intensify the total effect of her work and its artistic and thematic unity. I would like to state again that the Baroque *comedia*, whose surface appears supercharged with images, secondary actions, and multiple mutually reinforcing literary figures, could only succeed and maintain itself as an artistic work because the basic structure underlying it is symmetrical, simple, and, accordingly, of great strength.

Francisco Antonio de Bances y López-Candamo (1662–1704)

Francisco de Bances Candamo, as he is generally known, was born in Asturias but educated in Seville where he became Doctor of Canon Law. He left Seville for Madrid in search of better opportunities there. His play *Por su Rey y por su dama* [For His King and His Lady] was performed at the Buen Retiro in 1685. His dramatic work was appreciated and, probably as the result of the success of his court plays, he was named to be official playwright to King Charles II in 1687, a post he resigned after only a few years, in 1693 or 1694. He then served as a treasury official in the provinces, except for one more brief period in Madrid where he again worked as a dramatist.

Besides the important critical work discussed briefly in the introduction to this chapter, Bances Candamo's theater (we have left to us the texts of twenty or so plays) is infused with the politics of the time. Moir and Wilson cite this political tendency of his works as a possible cause for his rather abrupt departure from the theatrical scene in Madrid. Of his work as a whole, they add that he "wrote his plays carefully, and most of them are good drama."[26] They continue by citing the appreciation of his work by the eighteenth-century critic Luzán, whose criticism of other Golden Age playwrights was generally much more acerbic in tone. Luzán praises Bances Candamo's work "for his wit, his elegant style, the good taste of his topics, and for the great care shown for verisimilitude, decorum and propriety of the actions and the people."[27]

For His King and His Lady.[28]   The plot of this, the first of Bances Candamo's plays to have had documented performance, is based on the historic taking of Amiens by Spanish troops through the use of subterfuge and audacity, in a strange mixture, under the leadership of Hernán Tello Portocarrero in 1597. Perhaps because of that basis in a theme of war, the play is characterized by overly long narrative speeches describing the action and very little dramatic action on stage. Just as possible an explanation for these descriptive passages and for the resulting simplicity in plot structures might be found in Bances Candamo's lack of experience in writing plays. However that may be, the play, that for modern tastes is one that deserves to be appreciated less, remained as one of his most popular works throughout the eighteenth and into the nineteenth centuries, a popularity that is witnessed by repeated printings.

Act I. Portocarrero is in Flanders, where he has become known as an audacious military leader as well as a man successful with the ladies. In a recent battle he has acquired the portrait of an intriguingly beautiful lady. He and his men await the arrival, under seal of safe passage granted in the recent truce, of Ernesto, the new governor of Amiens *(ex)*. Ernesto arrives with his daughter Serafina, the lady of the portrait. This she recovers from Portocarrero together with his offer to reclaim it from her even in the midst of enemy held territory *(in)*. He escorts the two to the frontier, where they are met by the French military leader, the Conde de San Pol, his wife, and Carlos, a former suitor of Serafina *(ra)*. When her coach overturns, the Conde, Carlos, and Portocarrero all rush to her aid. Portocarrero is recognized and only his daring and bravery allow him to escape *(ra)*.

Act II. At a masked ball being given at Carnival time in Amiens, Madame de San Pol loses her mask and all others must, out of courtesy, then unmask. Serafina's two suitors are, as a result, recognized as the Conde de San Pol and Carlos. This gives rise to various feelings of jealousy and dislike *(ra)*. Portocarrero arrives in disguise and dances with Serafina who agrees to meet him later at her balcony with the portrait he has come to reclaim *(ra)*. Having been unmasked, the ladies exchange costumes for the continuation of the ball at the palace. The Conde and Carlos, both jealous of Serafina's attentions, make an excuse to quarrel and one of the Conde's servants falls victim to Carlos's sword *(pp)*. Portocarrero is still waiting for Serafina, who has been delayed by the quarrel, when Ernesto, following the murder, tries to arrest him. In the dark, Ernesto is wounded, and Portocarrero escapes. He and Carlos exchange costumes, each one believing that the exchange will guarantee his own safety. Both, then, return to the ball; both are arrested; and both are unmasked to everyone's surprise *(pt)*. Portocarrero's servant douses the lights while his master escapes into the safety of Serafina's room and arms. She agrees to marry him whenever their two cities are under the flag of one king *(rt)*.

Act III. Portocarrero develops an audacious but workable plan to take Amiens *(rt)*. Carlos, whose aim is still the hand of Serafina as well as revenge against the Conde, comes to help *(pt)*. As the Conde and Ernesto dispute the relative powers of civil and military governments, the attack is made and the city taken *(rt)*. Ernesto surrenders the city to the Spanish troops and the Conde escapes to plan a counterattack *(ec)*. Portocarrero claims the hand of Serafina in marriage, banishes Carlos to another area, and orders an escort to return Madame de San Pol to her husband *(dt)*.

A review of the foregoing plot summary will reveal the weaknesses of this *comedia:* (1) overly wordy speeches in acts I and III that are symptomatic of the lack of dramatic action; and (2) most of the dramatic action of the work is limited to the second act that is punctuated by music and dancing. The virtues of the play are not as obvious but they lie in the fine poetry, well-drawn and interesting characterizations, and the witty use of *sententiae* to underscore the political criticisms for which Bances Candamo is known. A fine example of this is found in the third act in the argument between Ernesto and the Conde over their relative powers and the sources from which these derive. The passage is, however, too long to cite here. Two shorter examples are found in what Portocarrero has to say about a soldier's deeds: "If they turn out well, they are great feats; if they turn out badly, they are crazy actions" (384a). He also claims that they who aspire to heroism must first lose the fear caused by reasoned thought, he must flee from understanding. This point he illustrates by citing Cortés's actions in the conquest of Mexico.

El esclavo en grillos de oro [Slave in Bonds of Gold]. [29]   This, the first of a politically inspired trilogy, was first performed for King Charles II, probably in late 1692. The story that Bances Candamo uses to satirize the political situation of that time is based in Roman history of the time of Trajan, one of the Roman emperors born in Spain. Trajan, in order to teach the rebellious Camillus a lesson, obliged him to take on the duties of being Emperor. The rebel, worn out by the work involved, with no time to call his own, feeling the censure of the Roman people, incapable of governing well, and unable even to choose his own love, finally recognized his own incapacity for rule. He asked and was granted Trajan's forgiveness. The plot of the work has been compared both to Shakespeare's *Measure for Measure* and to Corneille's *Cinna,* but the political messages found in the play are strictly those that Bances Candamo wanted to get across to the King and to his audience.

Act I. The Emperor Trajano and his nephew Adriano return to triumph in Rome. Adriano, who had once courted the patrician Octavia, is now a competitor with Camilo for the attentions of Sirene *(ex).* Camilo plots with his aide Lidoro to assassinate Trajano and take power for himself before Adriano can be recognized as heir *(in).* Cleantes, Roman Consul and advisor to Trajano, warns the Emperor of the plot. Trajano, promising exemplary punishment for Camilo, orders his arrest *(ra).* Octavia and Sirene, separately, go to the palace garden for a walk at the same time that both Adriano and Camilo appear there in the hope of meeting Sirene. To a constant musical background, the couples become confused and alternately jealous *(ra).* The two young men are about to do battle when troops enter from both sides carrying torches. Frustrated in his attempt to arrest Adriano, Camilo decides to submit to the arrest ordered by Trajano peacefully, in the hope that a better opportunity to carry out his plan will still present itself *(ra).*

Act II. At a meeting of the Roman Senate, Camilo is tried and found guilty. Trying, however unsuccessfully, to forewarn Adriano of his true intentions, Trajano asks the Senate to approve Camilo as Caesar. This is approved for a trial period in which Trajano and Cleantes are to advise him in his duties. If Camilo thus succeeds, he will be confirmed in office *(ra).* Octavia, who had looked forward to marriage to Adriano and to becoming Empress, is greatly disappointed; Sirene, who had hoped to marry Camilo, realizes the inequality of stations, and accepts the hopeless nature of her love with strength, sadness and stoic resignation *(ra).* Camilo holds his first audience along with Trajano but is surprised to find that matters are not always as simple as they seem *(ra).* After several such experiences dealing with a musician, an alchemist, and a woman, Camilo finally exclaims his surprise at his own ignorance *(pp).* There follows a petition from a poet whose satires against the government have got him in trouble. Again Camilo errs in his judgment of the case *(rt)*. Camilo seeks respite from arduous duty in the garden where he runs into Sirene who, in spite of her continuing love for him, rejects his advances on the ground that he has a higher duty to the state *(pt)*. Cleantes enters to reinforce this point as well as to call him back to his desk and duty *(rt)*. An interview between Adriano and Sirene is overheard by Octavia, who had been looking for him in order to console him over Camilo's rise, and by Camilo, who must hear Sirene boldly state her intent of forgetting him *(pt)*. A wrestling match between Camilo and Adriano results in a draw as Trajano calls Camilo back to work. Camilo at last realizes that he has become a slave not only to duty but to his own ambition *(rt)*.

Act III. As Camilo is occupied with the paper work of the Empire, Cleantes brings three successive problems to him: (1) There is a need, despite the nearly empty treasury, to pay for a public celebration where he is to be recognized as Caesar. (2) The same money is needed to finance a counterattack on rebellious Britain if only to prevent the rebellion from spreading to Germany and the Lowlands. (3) He should approve the request of Adriano to marry Sirene *(pt)*. Sirene seeks the comfort of consolation in Octavia, but she, angry at Adriano's attentions to Sirene, adds salt to the wounds by pointing out that Sirene is accepting Octavia's left-overs *(rt)*. Camilo again comes to talk with Sirene and is, again, rejected, but his obvious love and dismay nearly convince her to give in. She is prevented from doing so by the entrance of Adriano, whose delicate treatment of the situation is absolutely correct as it placates Camilo and at the same time Adriano achieves his purpose *(pt)*. Trajano finally makes his intent clear to Adriano. In a soliloquy Camilo, worried over the state of matters, decides that he would rather not be Emperor but can't quite bring himself, yet, to make the break *(rt)*. This musing is interrupted by three disturbing events: (1) News arrives from Adriano's army that is fast approaching Rome in his behalf; (2) There are new uprisings in Sicily and Sardinia; and (3) Music is played indicating the upcoming wedding of Sirene and Adriano. All this happens just as Camilo is to appear before the Senate for confirmation in office *(ec)*. Instead, he abdicates in Trajano's favor; Sirene agrees to accept Camilo as husband; and Adriano, now official heir to the Empire, agrees to allow that marriage accepting Octavia as his own bride *(dt)*.

Structurally, poetically, and dramatically the best of Bances Candamo's *comedias,* this play is admirably suited to the exposition of the political thesis at its core. As a dramatization of the education-of-a-prince theme the piece works well on the stage and still fits within the artistic mold of its time. Practically every dramatic moment is aimed at showing the prince at the service of the state, how he must act prudently at all times to ensure the safety and continuance of the state, or how he must always be aware of the motives behind every petition, behind all advice that he receives. Even Camilo eventually becomes aware of the blind ambition (and the insufficiency of this) behind his own desire for power. He also realizes the same quality as being behind the bad advice given to him by his own flattering supporters. Finally, he recognizes the extent to which the ruler becomes subject to the state, indeed so subject that Camilo refuses the honor. He will not be a slave even in golden chains, even if it is just this slavery on the part of a good leader that ensures the freedom of his vassals. Throughout the play, the speeches are spiced with sententiae commenting on palace politics. These can be shown to be related to the situation in Spain during the last decade of the seventeenth century. The importance, however, of the work does not lie in its contemporary relevance but in the universal vision of the problems of a good political leader, a transcendental message that Bances Candamo succeeded in presenting while managing to avoid even the appearance of being overly didactic.

In part this is achieved by the use of such reinforcing techniques as the music that serves as a background for much of the action and in part by the interesting and elaborate staging. One of the first things an inveterate reader of *comedias* would notice about this one is that the stage directions are very complete and detailed (contrary to the sketchy, often lacking directions found in early *comedias,* an aspect that frequently causes difficulty for the neophyte reader). These directions are, of course, partly the result of the fact that the play was prepared for palace performance and partly because of the pageantry being staged: a Roman triumph, a meeting of the Roman Senate. But, they are also undeniably the result, in part, of a greater desire on the part of the author to play a more active, creative role in the production of his own work in the theater.

Of the greatest interest in *Slave in Bonds of Gold* is the characterization of the various persons taking a main part in the drama. Particularly because this aspect is often attacked as one of the weak spots in the *comedia*, the extent of and the delicacy with which Bances Candamo develops his characters here is of great interest.

The character of Camilo is of highest interest because if he is not realized as a sympathetic character, in spite of his treachery and the ambition that bring him to seek power, if his renunciation of power at the end is not truly verisimile, we would have to reject the whole play. It is, then, precisely because of the perfection achieved in the development of his character that this *comedia* works well. From the moment of our first acquaintance with Camilo, our feelings toward him (his character) are ambivalent since those qualities are in conflict with the treacherous acts he plots. After setting up the rebellion against Trajano and Adriano, with whom the audience feels a natural sympathy after the opening scene where the two are received in triumph, Camilo attempts to justify his plans by following the very human process of rationalization: (1) Such a daring act is good or evil depending on whether or not it succeeds. (2) An example is found in a tale about Alexander the Great, who had to admit, in all honesty, that he was a greater, even if more successful, thief than a pirate who was called to justice before him. (3) If the gods helped him in gaining power, how could they then find him guilty of sin in doing so? (4) He was descended from Roman nobility and was, therefore, better suited to rule the Empire than either Trajano or Adriano, relatively new arrivals from Spain. This process, one that tends to humanize him for an audience at first disposed to feel disgust at his treason, is accompanied by the exposition of two new sides to his character, each of which would seem to lead the audience into sympathy with him: first, he wants the throne, principally, to be able to lay the world at the feet of his beloved Sirene, and, second, he has rewarded the past loyalty of his slave Gelanor by freeing him. If this generosity is not returned with gratitude, it was at least a noble gesture.

Another necessary element in the development of the character of Camilo is the prudence he demonstrates when his arrest is ordered by Trajano. In spite of the fact that he is accompanied by sufficient force to resist arrest, he wisely postpones any action that would precipitate his carefully planned rebellion before it would succeed by means of its own strength. Therefore, he orders his men to submit and goes with the arresting force to find out exactly what Trajano has in mind. Moreover, and just as needed as any of the above to attract the sympathy of the audience to Camilo, is the fact that his love for Sirene is consistently drawn as being a very real one. In contrast to the standard gallant of the *comedia*, in fact in contrast to the actions of Adriano, Camilo never once varies in his love for Sirene; he never, even in the moments when she feels that she must reject him, wavers in his devotion. These consistently repeated qualities in Camilo's character (intelligence, nobility, generosity, prudence, humanity, and love) are the very qualities that lend verisimilitude to his final abdication, one that he justifies by his realization that a good leader needs to be a super being. He must serve unselfishly and have the ability to detach himself from others as well as from the consequences of his acts. Camilo realizes that the motives that incited him to seek power were not the proper ones. He can neither serve the good of the state unselfishly nor can the power give him what he wants.

Although Bances Candamo has paid the same careful attention to the development of the characters of Trajano and Adriano, even more noteworthy is the work with the two ladies Sirene and Octavia, who here take on the three-dimensional appearance of real women who react as they should and would in the circumstances given, even in the very limited number of times they appear on stage. In the first act the two women take very unimportant roles: Octavia loves Adriano, Sirene loves Camilo and, in the final scene, they are both given reason for jealousy. In the second act their respective characters begin to emerge and Sirene takes on the role of first *dama*. She shows great emotion when Camilo is found guilty at his trial before the senate. When the strange sentence is passed, she is relieved but at the realization of what his rise to power means to their relationship she is nearly overcome. Her speech to Camilo rejecting his love and his continued attention to her is a masterpiece of propriety. Octavia, on the other hand, wants to console Adriano because of his dashed hopes but finds herself fearing the possibility that she might be placed in a social position beneath that of her rival Sirene. In the third act, the characterization of the two ladies is completed and Sirene certainly emerges as the more sympathetic of the pair, Octavia as the more human. Sirene first tells Adriano that his good wishes are not needed since she cannot hope to marry Camilo. She will not, however, accept his attentions. Octavia, overcome by anger and jealousy when the marriage proposed by Adriano to Sirene (through her family) is approved, screams at the humble Sirene that she is welcome to her left-over suitors. When Camilo again approaches Sirene and is again rejected, he hints that he will have Adriano killed rather than allow the wedding to proceed. Sirene's plea for Adriano's life brings on Camilo's last desperate attempt to gain her hand, an attempt that is once again frustrated.

Clearly Sirene is the better of the two women even though Octavia comes out as more human in her reactions. Sirene is self-effacing, unselfish, faithful, and humble. Octavia is proud, jealous, disdainful, and real. In the end Sirene gets the man she loved, as does Octavia: Sirene because she deserves to be rewarded. It is interesting to note that, insofar as characteristic qualities are concerned, each lady marries her opposite.

Bances Candamo's other plays merit more study than they have as yet been given. Two other easily accessible plays are just as interesting, but for different reasons. His *El duelo contra su dama* [Duel with His Lady][30] is a late-blooming member of that well-worn *comedia* type dealing with the lady who disguises herself as a man and goes off to seek redress against the lover who has abandoned her for another. The other is the equally interesting reworking of Belmonte Bermúdez's *The Tailor from Campillo.*[31] In reworking the play, Bances Candamo gives it much greater dramatic unity, heightens the political import of the work, eliminates elements that in the later period would be seen to be in bad taste, and reduces the hectic, disarranged action of the earlier version to a more stable, more easily realized drama.

The last fifty years of the seventeenth century (1651–1700) were not dead ones for the *comedia*. Things, interesting things, were happening in the works of the best writers of the period even as the work of other poetasters and mimics of earlier works abounded making use of the easily discovered formula for the rapid production of the plays needed to make the public believe that there was always something new to be seen in the theater.

To summarize the changes in this final period, I would have to cite the following:

(1) *The increasing frequency of the preparation of plays for the theater by reworking earlier pieces chosen from the whole range of the "comedia."* For a

variety of reasons, some economic, some practical, and some aesthetic, the later playwrights plagiarized (in modern terms) the work of earlier dramatists, a practice that was not considered at all dishonest at the time. There seem to be no special reasons for which plays were chosen for such *refundición*. The best known works of the most famous playwrights were as likely to be reworked as were the least known pieces of the minor dramatists. A need to have a text to sell, the pressure of the time needed to produce a completely new work, the desire to rewrite a play to fit the strengths and abilities of a specific acting company, or a wish to bring the *comedia* into conformity with current aesthetic or censorial taste, all operated in the growth of this practice, a process that was to follow the genre well into the eighteenth century.

(2) *The new importance, relatively, of two "comedia" types: the "comedia de figurón" and the mythological drama.* The *figurón* plays developed as a natural consequence of the importance placed in the later plays on the process of characterization and of the movement of the *comedia* toward a more social mode as expressed in satire of the foibles of mankind. These plays were certainly most successfully produced in the public and provincial theaters that lacked the complicated stage machinery found in the palace theaters (some of which were also open to the public). The machinery needed for the production of mythological drama was as much a visual and aural experience as it was a dramatic one. It is as if the theater were moving toward two extremes at once: the black satire of human eccentricities as found in the real world and the shining beauty of poetic myth found in an idealized world.

(3) *The further development of theatrical procedures designed to enhance the appeal of the dramatic experience.* In this final period of the century, the writers began to make freer use of music and dance as elements of the plot structures. Some works, indeed, make such free use of the other arts that they can no longer be classified as *comedias* and, therefore, pass beyond the bounds of the present study. As the theater audience, through constant contact with the highly stylized rhetorical language of the *comedia*, became more sophisticated poetically, the authors made greater use of that language in an attempt to demonstrate their ability at verbal pyrotechnics. Sometimes that show of poetic brilliance seems to have become an end in itself and, except for the music and dance, the plays might become bogged down in their own verbosity. The theater became a self-conscious one. The later plays are filled with commentary

on the works themselves as theater or on a particular bit of action as theater. Increasingly, the actors comment to the audience on the action or even demand that the audience participate actively in the theatrical experience. One final aspect of the development of stage procedures is that the authors themselves seem to show a greater interest in the production of their dramas. This is evidenced by the presence, in the manuscripts and texts, of increasingly detailed stage directions. This may be due, in part, to the fact that the authors were increasingly in actual command of the production of their own works, especially those prepared for presentation at court.

(4) *A continued refinement of the structural principles guiding the composition of "comedias."* The same basic dramatic plan that had been used since the formation of the *comedia* as a literary genre was still in use; however, there was a notable tendency, in this final fifty-year period, toward a simplification of plot, and toward the use of a symmetrical arrangement of dramatic episodes in such a way as to underscore the basic thematic unity of the play or to emphasize the thesis it presented. In addition, the later plays tended to present more complex actions through the use of expository techniques or narrations rather than by means of dramatic action. The narrations so presented often evolved into long, poetically involved segments intended as displays of the poet's technique as much as for the material they contained. They often give nearly the appearance of being "set pieces" within the framework of the dramatic action. In modern terms, they would slow the play to the point of boredom but for an audience capable of appreciating them as works of art in and of themselves, they must have been quite meaningful. Nothing speaks more clearly for the increasing evolution of the *comedia* toward a ritual act than does this aspect of the late *comedias*.

(5) *A definite tendency to move away from the exuberant freedom of the Baroque toward the more strictly controlled norms of the Neoclassic style.* Certain qualities generally cited as typical of neoclassic theater have been cited above as appearing with increasing strength and frequency during the last years of the century that concerns us here. Although the Aristotelian unities of action, place, and time were under critical discussion throughout the seventeenth century and certain *preceptistas* (makers of critical law) had been clamoring for their acceptance since the first years, it was only in the last half of that period that consistent,

meaningful efforts were made by serious dramatists to bring the *comedia* into harmony with them.[32] Additionally, the principles of decorum and good taste (as noted in the theoretical work of Bances Candamo) came into full play during this period. One need only cite the action of such earlier plays as Miguel Sánchez's *The Careful Guard* or compare the original of Belmonte Bermúdez's *The Tailor from Campillo* with its reworking by Bances Candamo to be certain of these changes. We have also seen how continual efforts were being made to perfect not only the dramatic form and the language used to present it but also to put increased emphasis on the didactic purpose of the drama. All of these qualities (adherence to the dramatic unities, attention paid to the principles of *decorum* and good taste, importance placed on the perfection of structure and language, and emphasis on the didactic purpose) are basically qualities of Neoclassic drama.

None of these qualities is absolutely new to this later period. All had been known and used to some extent by earlier writers, as I have shown here; however, their growth in the last half of the seventeenth century speaks strongly for a gradual and independent movement toward that newer style rather than the sudden imposition of those norms under the influence of the Frenchified courts of the Bourbon dynasty of the eighteenth century.

Chapter Six
The Significance of the Minor Dramatists

The works of the minor dramatists undoubtedly reflect the dramatic trends and the evolutionary forces that impinged upon them more clearly than do the *comedias* of the better-known playwrights. This is true in part because the lesser-known writers were (as is the case for relatively unknown writers in any age) under greater pressure to please their audience whether that was the public who attended functions in the *corrales* or the members of high society who were welcomed into palace theaters. In part also, they were constrained to attract the attention and financial support of the producer-directors (or wealthy patrons) who were the market to whom the plays were sold. These pressures are reflected in their works in two ways: either as an exaggeration of the most successful theatrical elements employed by the major writers (that is those elements found to have the greatest audience appeal) or as a reaction to the triteness of repeatedly used materials and techniques. Demonstrably, then, a better view of *"what, when, why, and how* the *comedia* was"* is to be found in these lesser-known works than in the few dozen plays, written by the ten major playwrights, that are too often the only contact even a scholar of Spanish literature ever has with that genre, probably the most distinctive and original literary offering of Spain's Golden Age.

Since the artistic experience of the theater results from the interaction of poet, director, actor, physical facilities, and audience, and not from the text alone, I have attempted in the foregoing chapters to approach the matter from along three distinct critical paths: literary-formulistic, chronological, and sociohistoric.

In the introductory chapter, I attempted first to define a theoretical base for the structure of the *comedia,* seeking dramatic elements common to the genre as a means of understanding the birth, maturation, and decay of the *comedia* as an art form. In each succeeding chapter, the works of exemplary playwrights were studied with reference to this theoretical foundation. My conclusion is that it took time and practice for the *comedia* formula to take shape and to become recognized for what it was. As they became aware of its existence, the minor dramatists followed that recipe for their works as closely, even more closely in some cases, than did the major writers. They not only followed the formula but occasionally reacted to it in what seems an effort to devise newer, more distinctive, and individual accretions to the basic format. At times, the originality of the minor dramatists far surpasses that of the more commonly studied figures. This becomes particularly apparent when attention is paid either to the most or to the least successful of their inventions.

Second, the chronological arrangement of the chapters, besides giving support to the study of the dramatic evolution suggested above, forms a type of literary-historical study showing the true importance of the major playwrights of the period to have been their ability to consolidate, in a creative way, advances (or changes) made by others. In this way, all dramatists, and most especially the minor writers, are best studied as transitional figures connecting the main cycles of creative theatrical activity. The work of the early *Lopistas* (1600–1621) finds itself clearly reflected in the works Lope himself wrote in that period and later, as well as other writers of his "school." The work of his competitors (1621–1630) is best recognized in its effects on the theater of Tirso de Molina, Mira de Amescua, and Ruiz de Alarcón. The "Calderonian" writers, Calderón de la Barca himself, Rojas Zorrilla, Moreto, Vélez de Guevara, and Pérez de Montalván, show the influence of their minor competitors (1631–1650). And, finally, the long period of generic decline (1651–1700) is beautifully punctuated by the best works of some minor writers whose works point the way into an uncertain future. A casual glance at the listings given here for the "also-rans," those minor dramatists whose work is not studied here (not for lack of interest but for lack of space), will show at least two other facts of interest: (1) As the century progresses, the number of writers seems to increase in geometrical proportion to the decrease in the number of plays each wrote. In other words, the number of *comedias* prepared for consumption in any one period of time (except for those years when the theaters were closed by royal fiat) seems to remain constant while the number of poets preparing those texts increases greatly. (2) There also seems to be a very real shift, although gradual and never complete, away from *comedias* written for original production in the public theaters toward works prepared by members of the court for first showing in the palace theaters. There is no doubt in my mind that these two facts are connected and that they result from socioeconomic factors that are not the subject of this study.

Third, since drama only comes into existence in the theater through the interaction of author, producer, actors, and audience, no literary genre is as receptive as is drama to changes in artistic fads or to the social, economic, and political developments that surround it. The minor writers are, at least theoretically, more responsive to those forces than are the more important, better established, and more independent major writers. Consequently, their works show more clearly the influence on them of changes in political power, the opening and closings of public and court theaters, and the relative sophistication of their audiences. That sophistication results not only from differences in social level but also from long years of contact with the language and the dramatic conventions employed in the theater. The works of the minor dramatists demonstrate even more clearly than do those of others the effects of the shift from theater as an entertainment for untutored masses to its acceptance as a ritualistic, auditory and visual spectacle set in an artistically solidified theatrical mold. Interestingly, as the plays became ever more closely structured and ritualistic in nature, the genre seems to have fractured into its separate components and, in its very death throes, to have given birth to new forms of pageantry, masque, and *zarzuela* ("opera").

It is difficult to specify with absolute accuracy the important "inventions" of any specific minor dramatists, yet I have cited certain writers as examples of what seems to have been happening in the theater at a given time. Among those I have written of as "early Lopistas," Miguel Sánchez certainly raised the technique of dramatic irony to an exciting level, so much so that Lope himself commented on Sánchez's skill in that regard. Certainly, ever after, the *comedia* shows the effects of Sánchez's work with "deception through truth." Salucio del Poyo brought to the theater not only historical matter that had until then been ignored as a source of drama, but also the great consuming theme of fortune that informs his works, plays that were cannibalized by later and more important writers for materials from which to build their own works. The plays of Andrés de Claramonte, as one of the earliest producer-writers, show a greatly improved knowledge of how the theater audience, playwright, and actors all interact to produce the dramatic experience. In addition to these specifics, their works as a whole show a characteristic interest in action over the poetry through which that action is expressed and a general inability to structure their plays into a single dramatic unit. At the time they were writing their plays, the *comedia* was still in its formative stages. Its recipe had not yet been completely formulated or tried.

The minor playwrights among the "challengers of Lope de Vega" are more successful in structuring their plays into artistically unified pieces. Felipe Godínez is perhaps best remembered for the balanced, symmetrical structures he achieved in his plays. Even though the way in which he built some of his works may seem, at times, somewhat mechanical, others show the dramatic structuring to work beautifully as a means of understanding the themes and theses he was putting forth. Diego Jiménez de Enciso, more than any other of the minor dramatists, managed to fit the historical materials so favored by the audiences of his day within the confines of a true dramatic structure. Although in his *Juan Latino* he does employ the plot and subplot arrangement so generally used by other writers of his time as a means of maintaining dramatic tension (e.g., the structure of Lope de Vega's *Fuenteovejuna*), in his *Prince Charles* and in *The Medicis of Florence* he makes great strides toward the creation of true historical drama. In *Prince Charles,* rather than hide the historical conflict beneath contrasting layers of subplot, Jiménez de Enciso brings the genre (historical drama) to new artistic heights by focussing his work on the contrasting characters of Prince Charles and his father King Philip II. In his play on the Medicis, the poet again advances dramatic technique by ending each of the first two acts on a note of unresolved tension that is resolved only in the opening scenes of the following act. The importance of this way of doing things can only be fully appreciated in the context of the theater of the epoch and the fact that *comedias* were customarily presented with intervening interludes (sometimes related by theme or by contrast to the play itself) that tended to interrupt the flow of the drama being presented. To a greater extent than any of the earlier dramatists, Luis de Belmonte Bermúdez, besides lifting dramatic irony to new heights as a comic device, realized the importance of the opening scene as an attention-grabbing strategem necessary to bring the usually unruly audience for whom he wrote under the control of the stage and, thus, under the spell of his drama.

Those dramatists who wrote in competition with Pedro Calderón, and with some of the finest of Spain's Golden Age dramatists, certainly followed the trends of the times in further simplifying the structure of their plays, making use of the formal, stylized poetic language of the Baroque, developing dramatic characterization to a higher level, and approaching their work from a more serious point of view. The most obvious contribution to the theater made by the court poet Antonio Hurtado de Mendoza was his consistent use of plots of socially significant themes: the social climber's use of wealth as a means of gaining acceptance; the roguish veterans who, on returning from foreign wars, depend on their wits and any opportunities presented to them as a means of gaining a living; and the problems of an unhappy marriage that can only be resolved by divorce. In each of Hurtado's plays, the characterization is so carefully and well handled, so interesting in itself, that the theme is (and properly so) practically subliminal though unmistakable. Alvaro Cubillo de Aragón is most interesting for the steps he took to simplify the structure of the *comedia,* practically eliminating the subplot as a technique for providing complications or dramatic tension. He did this both in his original works and in those he rewrote from earlier models.

The last fifty years of the century saw a great proliferation in the number of writers preparing texts for performance. These dramatists, as did even earlier writers, rewrote existing *comedias* in addition to preparing works of their own, generally of the same familiar types so long in use. Yet, the growth in number and in kind of two special classes of plays (the comic *comedia de figurón* and the showy mythological drama) was most notable. Agustín de Salazar y Torres openly employed his audience's probable knowledge of Spanish literature and of recent history in his plays. He also made heavy use of dramatic convention as the stuff from which to create humor. This is best seen in the constant reference made by characters in his plays to the fact that they are, after all, only figments of the theatrical world. Sor Juana Inés must be cited for the manner in which her plays are structured in a perfectly symmetrical mode as well as for the novel, inventive way in which she applied conventional symbolism: bringing light onto the stage creates chaos while putting the lights out leads to a proper resolution of the problem, an escape from the labyrinth muddles matters, a return to the maze clears them up. Francisco de Bances Candamo deserves recognition for the perfection and the three-dimensional quality of the characters in his plays. They, like all real humans, have weaknesses and strengths, attractive as well as repulsive qualities, that act in concert to create lifelike personalities. The works of all three of these playwrights exhibit certain qualities in common: an increased use of music, dance, and the other arts as adjuncts to the drama: and a gradual movement towards the acceptance of the theatrical norms that were to govern the drama of the following century. We can, indeed, find in their plays some of the very qualities that became the hallmarks of Neoclassic theater. These are the same attributes cited by Ignacio Luzán, the outstanding critic of the period, when he praised the drama of Bances Candamo: perfection of style, good taste, verisimilitude, and decorum and propriety of both action and character.

What I have had to say here is meant to be taken as opinion, a personal view limited by the amount of contact and study I have had time to accomplish since becoming interested in the minor dramatists. As such it is subject to new interpretations and to increasing knowledge. The lack of critical studies devoted to the works of these lesser-known figures and works has hampered this investigation and is, without exaggeration, shocking in view of the many beauties and the myriad interesting elements found in their plays. While I am constrained to recognize that some of their dramas (including some of those studied here) are imperfect, even faulty or outright poor theater, some others of their *comedias* are most interesting and quite illustrative of the literary and aesthetic currents that affected the theatrical art of the times. It is just as true that some plays by the minor dramatists far surpass in quality the majority of the works that are studied by critics of the *comedia* solely because they were written by a more important dramatist. With the possible exception of Sor Juana Inés de la Cruz, not one of these writers has achieved the recognition or critical study that his dramatic works merit. I hear the loudest cries for attention coming from the works of the unjustly neglected Felipe Godínez, Diego Jiménez de Enciso, and Francisco de Bances Candamo. Other critics who enter into this field will be attracted to their works or even to the theater of their competitors among the more than 150 writers of *comedias* of the seventeenth century, most of whom are not even mentioned by name in this study.

I hope, then, that I have shown the following: (1) that the basic qualities of the genre we know as the *comedia* are more readily observed in the works of the lesser-known dramatists than in those of the better established playwrights; (2) that each of the minor dramatists studied here (and many who are not) made unique and valuable contributions to the development of the genre; (3) that the *comedia* is best viewed, not as a group of works centered around the leaders (Lope and Calderón) of two schools whose works were so innovative that they were the model that others followed, but rather as a continuing process of development and composition to which all contributed and that the works of these two major figures represent the evolutionary state of the genre at the time they were written; and (4) that, as is best seen in the shift away from the open, free-swinging early *comedias* toward the highly stylized, strictly structured works of the final years of the century, the *comedia* format gradually became more static, nearly petrified to the point where it no longer was as responsive as it once had been to the purposes for which drama was written. More than anything else, this resulted in the demise of the *comedia* as an art form, one that died giving birth to the theatrical art of the new century.

Notes and References

Chapter One

1. Gustav Freytag, *Technique of the Drama*, tr. E. J. MacEwen (New York: B. Blom, 1968), p. 3.
2. Ibid., pp. 104–105.
3. Frank H. O'Hara, *A Handbook of Drama* (New York: Willet Clark and Co., 1938), pp. 130–33.
4. Ibid., pp. 132–33.
5. William F. Thrall and Addison Hibbard, *A Handbook to Literature* (New York: Odyssey, 1960), p. 356. See also the complete entries under *conflict* (pp. 104–105) and *plot* (pp. 356–58).
6. Another description of this same process, but one that does not use the same terminology, is to be found in William Gibson, *Shakespeare's Game* (New York: Atheneum, 1978). I do not use Gibson's vocabulary here because it is too far removed from standard critical usage. Gibson is a playwright himself describing the techniques, and makes no pretense to the observance of standard literary criticism.
7. Lope de Vega Carpio, *El arte nuevo de hacer comedias* [New Art of Writing Plays], line 174. Any standard version of the text may be referred to, but one commonly available text is that published by Austral (*El arte nuevo de hacer comedias. La discreta enamorada.* Colección Austral, no. 842). This and all other translations from the Spanish are my own. Hereafter, in the interest of conserving space, only the location of the quotation will be noted, within the body of the text if that procedure is clear enough. No attempt will be made to provide the original Spanish text here.
8. Typical of this treatment of the play's structure are two articles: Edward M. Wilson, "Images et structures dans *Peribáñez*, tr. C. V. Auburn , *Bulletin Hispanique* 51 (1949): 125–59 (see especially pp. 151ff.), and Gustavo Correa, "El doble aspecto de la honra en *Peribáñez y el Comendador de Ocaña*," *Hispanic Review* 26 (1958): 188–99. Neither critic even deals with the scenes of the play that follow the death of the Comendador.
9. The phenomenon explained here is remarkably uniform for recent *comedia* criticism as exemplified in several of the most basic treatises relating to it (Bruce W. Wardropper, "The Implicit Craft of the Spanish *Comedia*," *Studies in Spanish Literature of the Golden Age Presented to Edward M. Wilson*, ed. R. C. Jones [London: Támesis, 1973], pp. 339–56; Arnold G. Reichen-

berger, "The Uniqueness of the *Comedia,*" [two articles of the same title], *Hispanic Review* 27 [1959]: 303–16, and 38 [1970]: 163–73; and Eric Bentley, "The *Comedia:* Universality or Uniqueness?" *Hispanic Review* 38 [1970]: 147–62). All three discuss the *comedia* as if it were a single genre, in terms of plots, protagonists, themes, and artistic unity. A. A. Parker, in his two majestic discussions, carefully avoids the issue I raise here. Not once, in either of his studies of the Spanish drama of the Golden Age ("The Approach to the Spanish Drama of the Golden Age," *Tulane Drama Review* 4 [1959]: 42–59; "The Spanish Drama of the Golden Age: A Method of Analysis and Interpretation," in *The Great Playwrights,* ed. Eric Bentley [New York: Doubleday, 1970], pp. 679–707), does he even use the word *comedia.* He writes of the *drama,* discussing only plays that may properly be so classified.

10. *Obras de Lope de Vega,* VI, ed. Marcelino Menéndez y Pelayo (Madrid: Real Academia de la Lengua, 1896), pp. l–li.

11. *Carlos V en Francia,* ed. Arnold G. Reichenberger (Philadelphia: University of Pennsylvania Press, 1962), pp. 32–34.

12. *Obras de Lope de Vega,* VI, p. clv.

13. S. Griswold Morley and Courtney Bruerton, *Cronología de las Comedias de Lope de Vega* (Madrid: Gredos, 1968), p. 235.

14. *Las paces de los reyes y la judía de Toledo,* ed. James A. Castañeda (Chapel Hill: University of North Carolina Press, 1962), p. 59.

15. "The Spanish Drama of the Golden Age. . . ," (see note 9), p. 696.

16. David H. Darst, "The Unity of *Las paces de los reyes y judía de Toledo,*" *Symposium* 25 (1971): 225–35. William C. McCrary, "Plot, Action, and Imitation: The Art of Lope's *Las paces de los reyes,*" *Hispanófila* 48 (1973): 1–17, especially p. 3, as quoted. Still one other study of this play has recently come to my attention, Lilia Paz da Strout, "Alfonso VIII como *persona* de Lope en *Las paces de los reyes y judía de Toledo,*" in *Studies in Language and Literature, The Proceedings of the Twenty-third Mountain Interstate Foreign Language Conference,* ed. Charles L. Nelson (Richmond: Eastern Kentucky University Press, 1976), pp. 481–88.

17. David Gitlitz, "Lyric Imagery and Structural Unity in Lope de Vega's *Paces de los reyes,*" paper presented at the annual conference of the Central Renaissance Association, February 1977, St. Louis, Missouri. E. M. Wilson and Duncan Moir, *The Golden Age: Drama 1492–1700* (London: Barnes and Noble, 1971), pp. 60–61.

18. Darst, p. 229.

19. The *comedias* were, after all, written to be performed and we must never lose sight of this aspect of the theater where playwrights, directors, actors, stage facilities, and audience all interreact in the production of the

piece. However, the role played by the public in such a performance is much less actively creative than that played by a reader who must mentally recreate as he reads. From the earliest times, *comedias* were read as well as performed. Juan del Encina and Bartolomé de Torres Naharro published their dramatic works in the later fifteenth and early sixteenth centuries. It is through Joan Timoneda's publication of them that we know much of Lope de Rueda's dramatic pieces. Lope de Vega began to oversee the edition of his own plays when he noted the market for pirate editions of them (*Partes* IX to XX). In a contemporary manuscript version of Tirso de Molina's *La firmeza en la Hermosura* (Vatican Library, Barberini Collection) there is a description of how the gallant has a copy of a recent *comedia* prepared as a present for his lady, who does not wish to endanger her reputation by attending the theater.

20. For a discussion of the problem, see Alberto Porqueras Mayo, *El problema de la verdad poética en el siglo de oro* (Madrid: Ateneo, 1961).

21. *La casa del tahur,* ed. Vern G. Williamsen (Chapel Hill: University of North Carolina Department of Romance Languages, 1973). See the introduction, pp. 13–27.

22. *No hay dicha ni desdicha hasta la muerte,* ed. Vern G. Williamsen, Columbia: University of Missouri Press, 1971.

23. Vern G. Williamsen, "Poetic Truth in Two *Comedias: No hay dicha ni desdicha hasta la muerte* and *No hay mal que por bien no venga* [*Don Domingo de Don Blas*]," *Hispanófila* 45 (1972): 39–47. See also *Don Domingo de Don Blas,* ed. Vern G. Williamsen (Chapel Hill: University of North Carolina Department of Romance Languages, 1975), pp. 7–16.

24. *Arte nuevo de hacer comedias* (see note 7). Diego Marín, *La intriga secundaria en el teatro de Lope de Vega* (Mexico: Andrea, 1958), shows how Lope mixed history and fictional plots rather consistently.

25. Edward Hopper, "A Critical and Annotated Edition of Mira de Amescua's *La rueda de la fortuna,*" unpublished doctoral dissertation, University of Missouri, 1972, pp. 48–54.

26. Cf. Angel Valbuena Prat, *Mira de Amescua: Teatro I* (Madrid: Espasa Calpe, 1960), pp. xx–xxi.

27. This technique was rather thoroughly explored in a series of articles: Claude E. Anibal, "Voces del cielo," *Romanic Review* 18 (1925): 57–70; "Another Note on the 'Voces del cielo,'" *Romanic Review* 18 (1927): 246–52; Alexander Haggerty Krappe, "Notes on 'Voces del cielo,'" *Romanic Review* 17 (1926): 65–68; and 19 (1928): 154–56.

28. The later plays that are most easily accessible to the student are Mira's *Ejemplo mayor de la desdicha,* ed. Valbuena Prat in *Mira de Amescua: Teatro II* (Madrid: Espasa Calpe, 1960), *No hay dicha ni desdicha hasta la muerte* (see

note 23), and *La segunda de don Alvaro,* ed. Nellie Sánchez Arce (Mexico: Jus, 1960).

29. Tirso de Molina, *Los balcones de Madrid* (*BAE* 5, p. 566c) and Antonio Hurtado de Mendoza, *El marido hace mujer* (*BAE* 45, p. 423c).

30. R.D.F. Pring-Mill, in his valuable study "The Sententiousness of *Fuenteovejuna,*" *Tulane Drama Review* 7:1 (Fall 1962):5–37, approaches the problem I formulate here but does not relate his material to the elements of dramatic structure in the fashion I suggest as a possibility.

31. James F. Burke, "Dramatic Resolution in *La verdad sospechosa,*" *Renaissance and Reformation* 11 (1975):52–59.

32. William M. Whitby, "Rosaura's Role in the Structure of *La vida es sueño,*" *Hispanic Review* 28 (1960):16–26. Everett W. Hesse, "Analysis and Interpretation of the Play," in his *Pedro Calderón's "La vida es sueño"* (New York: C. Scribner's Sons, 1961), pp. 15–55.

33. Hopper studies these matters on pp. 54–61.

34. Vern G. Williamsen, "The Dramatic Function of *Cuentecillos* in Some Plays by Mira de Amesuca," *Hispania* 54 (1971):62–67.

35. Vern G. Williamsen, "The Structural Function of Polymetry in the Spanish *Comedia,*" in *Perspectivas de la Comedia,* ed. Alva V. Ebersole (Chapel Hill: University of North Carolina Department of Romance Languages, 1977), pp. 33–47; see particularly pp. 40–41.

36. See note 35.

Chapter Two

1. The fact is that, just as present-day television drama has become a vehicle for comment on and satire of contemporary life and society, the *comedia* performed that same function in the Spain of its day. Examples may easily be found in most of the articles written by Ruth Lee Kennedy, but the practice is particularly well summarized in her *Studies in Tirso I, The Dramatist and His Competitors, 1620–26* (Chapel Hill: University of North Carolina Department of Romance Languages, 1974).

2. This decrease in Lope's popularity is adequately demonstrated by the figures for his annual production of *comedias* in the years concerned. See S. G. Morley and C. Bruerton, *Cronología de las comedias de Lope de Vega* (Madrid: Gredos, 1968), either the table of dated works (pp. 44–73) or the chronological tables (pp. 590–606).

3. See the book dealing with these Valencian dramatists by John G. Weiger, *The Valencian Dramatists of Spain's Golden Age* (Boston: G. K. Hall, 1976).

4. These dramatists have been treated in the TWAS series. See William E. Wilson, *Guillén de Castro* (Boston: G. K. Hall, 1973); James A. Castañeda, *Mira de Amescua* (Boston: G. K. Hall, 1977); and Margaret Wilson, *Tirso de Molina* (Boston: G. K. Hall, 1977).

5. *Laurel de Apolo* in *Colección de las obras sueltas assí en prosa como en verso de Frey Lope Félix de Vega Carpio* (Madrid: Don Antonio de Sancha, 1776), 1:61–62.

6. *El viaje entretenido* (Madrid: Castalia, 1972), p. 164.

7. *Arte nuevo de hacer comedias*, vv. 319–22.

8. *Viaje del Parnaso* in *Obras completas* (Madrid: Aguilar, 1970), 1:80a.

9. *La Filomena*, in *Colección de las obras sueltas. . . ,* 2:371–467.

10. "Canción a Cristo Crucificado," in *Primera parte de las flores de poetas ilustres* (Valladolid, 1605) fols. 176r–178r; and "Oíd señor don Gaiferos," in *Romancero general* (Madrid: Juan Cuesta, 1604). The latter poem is reproduced in *BAE* 10:252–53.

11. Unedited manuscripts 16.729 and 16.832 of the National Library in Madrid. In spite of the facts that both manuscript versions are of the same play and attributed to Miguel Sánchez, and that the text of this play is in no way related to that of the play of the same title published with attribution to Juan Sánchez, Antonio and Julián Paz y Melia in the *Catálogo de las piezas manuscritas en la Biblioteca Nacional* (Madrid: Biblioteca Nacional, 1896 and 1934) claim that all three are identical and thus add to the confusion over the names of the authors.

12. Juan Sánchez wrote at a later time than did Miguel and was alive at least until the 1650s. In addition to the two plays by Juan Sánchez in the 1638 volume, we have a poem, *La vida y muerte de Judas Iscariote* ("The Life and Death of Judas Iscariot") of 1632, and another, *La vida de Epanimonides* ("The Life of Epanimonidas") of 1652.

13. *BAE* 43.

14. *"La isla bárbara" and "La guarda cuidadosa": Two "Comedias" by Miguel Sánchez (el Divino),* ed. Hugo A. Rennert (Boston: Ginn; Halle: S. M. Niemayer, 1896).

15. Ibid. See Rennert's remarks on the subject on page x and on page xix (particularly note 6). These show that he did not understand the operation of the process.

16. Manuscript 16.729 of the National Library (Madrid).

17. *BAE* 43:1–30.

18. These generalizations are made on the basis of the studies Morley and Bruerton prepared of Lope's versification habits (see note 2 above) and unpublished studies of Guillén de Castro's versification that I have made.

19. Justo García Soriano, "Damián Salustio del Poyo: Nuevos datos biográficos," *Boletín de la Real Academia Española* 13 (1926):269–82, 474–506.

20. Leipzig: Brockhaus, 1886.

21. *BAE* 43:437–89.

22. *Tercera parte de las comedias de Lope de Vega y otros autores* (Barcelona: Cormellas, 1612), fols. 150–66.

23. *Flor de las comedias de diferentes autores, Quinta parte* (Barcelona: Cormellas, 162), fols. 190–206.

24. Manuscript 14.960 of the National Library (Madrid).

25. *BAE* 43:xxxv.

26. *Parte XVII de las obras de Lope de Vega Carpio* (Madrid: Viuda de Alonso Martín, 1623). *Los muertos vivos* is the fourth play in this volume.

27. *La segunda de don Alvaro*, ed. Nellie E. Sánchez Arce (Mexico: Jus, 1960). The play was apparently written in the period 1621–24 and is available in the form of an autograph manuscript at the *Museo del Teatro* in Barcelona. The relationship between Salucio's play and the one by Mira de Amescua was studied by Leicester Bradner in "The Theme of *Privanza* in Spanish and English Drama, 1590–1625," *Homenaje a William L. Fichter* (Madrid: Castalia, 1971), pp. 97–106; see especially pp. 100–105.

28. Raymond R. MacCurdy, *"Tragic Harmatia* and *La próspera y adversa fortuna de don Alvaro de Luna,"* *Hispania* 47 (1964):82–90.

29. Karl C. Gregg, "The Probable Source of Tirso's Jewish Doctor," *Romance Notes* 17 (1976):302–304.

30. See Karl C. Gregg, "Del Poyo's Judás and Tirso's Don Juan," *Symposium* 29 (1975):345–60; and Vern G. Williamsen, "Tres grandes pecadores en el teatro de Salucio del Poyo, Lope de Vega, y Tirso de Molina," *Estudios* 31 (1975):73–86.

31. *El viaje entretenido*, p. 158.

32. Sturgis E. Leavitt, *The "Estrella de Sevilla" and Claramonte* (Cambridge, Mass.: Harvard University Press, 1931).

33. Gerald E. Wade in the Introduction to his edition of *El burlador de Sevilla* (New York: Charles Scribner's Sons, 1969), pp. 6–16.

34. Leavitt, p. 31.

35. *BAE* 43:491–509.

36. *BAE* 43:511–27.

37. Ed. A. Julián Valbuena Briones (Madrid: Espasa Calpe, 1956).

38. Unedited manuscripts in the National Library (Madrid), nos. 15.270 and 17.133.

39. *Segunda parte de comedias escogidas de las mejores de España* (Madrid: Imprenta Real, 1652), fols. 141r–158r.

40. Unedited manuscript 15.319 of the National Library (Madrid).

41. *Parte veynte y nueve*. *Doze comedias de Lope de Vega Carpio* (Huesca: Pedro Lusón, 1634).

42. For one explanation of this kind of action taking place on stage, see Sturgis E. Leavitt, "Strip-tease in Golden Age Drama," *Homenaje a Rodríguez Moñino* (Madrid: Castalia, 1966), 2:305–10.

43. *El viaje entretenido,* pp. 155–58.

Chapter Three

1. Hugo Rennert, *The Spanish Stage in the Time of Lope de Vega* (New York: Hispanic Society of America, 1909), pp. 230–32. Reprinted in part by Dover in New York, 1963.

2. N. D. Shergold, *A History of the Spanish Stage* (London: Oxford University Press, 1967), pp. 264–330.

3. As witness the descriptions as given in Tirso de Molina's *Los cigarrales de Toledo* of such private performances *(particulares),* or his own play on the Pizarro trilogy written for such performance while he was in Trujillo, the seat of the Pizarros, in 1626–1629.

4. These "major" dramatists are each the subject of a volume in the Twayne World Authors Series: Margaret Wilson, *Tirso de Molina* (1977), Walter Poesse, *Juan Ruiz de Alarcón* (1972), James A. Castañeda, *Mira de Amescua* (1977), Everett W. Hesse, *Calderón de la Barca* (1967), Raymond R. MacCurdy, *Francisco de Rojas Zorrilla* (1968), Jack H. Parker, *Juan Pérez de Montalván* (1975), and James A. Castañeda, *Agustín de Moreto* (1974).

5. Adolfo de Castro, "Noticias de la vida del Doctor Felipe Godínez," *Memorias de la Real Academia Española* 8 (1902):277–83.

6. Edward Glaser, "La comedia de Felipe Godínez, 'O el fraile ha de ser ladrón o el ladrón ha de ser fraile,'" *Revista de Literatura* (1957):91–107.

7. *Amán y Mardoqueo,* in *Quinta parte de comedias escogidas de los mejores ingenios de España* (Madrid: Pablo de Val, 1653), fols. 48–79.

8. *La traición contra su dueño,* ed. Thomas C. Turner (Chapel Hill, N.C.: Estudios de Hispanófila, 1975).

9. Arnold G. Reichenberger, in two articles with identical title, "The Uniqueness of the *Comedia,*" *Hispanic Review* 27 (1959):303–16; 38 (1970):163–73, deals extensively with the themes of faith and honor as bases of the *comedia*.

10. University of Missouri, 1970, pp. 63–79.

11. *Aun de noche alumbra el sol* in *BAE* 45:199–213.

12. *O el fraile ha de ser ladrón* in a *suelta* (Madrid: Sanz, 1743).

13. *San Mateo en Etiopía* (autograph manuscript not previously reported as such, number 15.701 of the National Library in Madrid); *El soldado del cielo, San Sebastián* (manuscript 14.988 of the National Library in Madrid); *De buen moro buen cristiano* (manuscript 16.437 of the National Library, Madrid); *La virgen de Guadalupe* (*suelta*, Sevilla: M. N. Vásquez, n.d.).

14. *Los trabajos de Job*, in *Parte Treinta una de las mejores comedias que hasta oy han salido* (Barcelona: Jaime Romeu, 1638), fols. 225–43; *La venganza de Tamar* (*suelta*, n.p., n.d.); Las *lágrimas de David* (*suelta*, Madrid: Manuel Sanz, n.d.)

15. *Ludovico el piadoso* (manuscript 17.076 of the National Library, Madrid); *Basta intentarlo* (manuscript 17.384 of the National Library, Madrid); *Acertar de tres la una* (a volume of collected plays, 41.IV.63 in the library of the Royal Academy of the Language, Madrid); *Los dos Carlos* (manuscript 18.074, fols. 249–311, of the National Library, Madrid); *Celos son bien y aventura*, in *Parte treinta y cinco de comedias nuevas escritas por los mejores ingenios de España* (Madrid: Bedmar, 1671), pp. 236–74.

16. The performance was carefully described by Antonio Hurtado de Mendoza (see our Chapter 4) in his *Convocación de las Cortes de Castilla y Juramento del Príncipe nuestro Señor, D. Baltasar Carlos, Primero deste nombre, año de 1632.*

17. *"El encubierto" y "Juan Latino." Dos comedias de Don Diego Ximénez de Enciso*, ed. Eduardo Juliá Martínez (Madrid: Real Academia Española, 1951).

18. There are several printings of *El príncipe don Carlos* with varying attributions. Apparently the *princeps* was in a volume of plays found in the Library of the University of Pennsylvania, *Las comedias del Fénix de España Lope de Vega Crapio* [*sic*]. *Parte veynte y cinco* (Barcelona: Sebastián Cormellas, 1631). That volume was first described by me in an article "Lope de Vega: A 'Missing' *Parte* and Two 'Lost' *Comedias*," *Bulletin of the Comediantes* 25 (1973):42–51; and again by Eugenio Asensio in "Textos nuevos de Lope de Vega en el Parte XXV extravagante (Zaragoza, 1631 [sic])," in *Homenaje a la memoria de don Antonio Rodríquez Moñino* (Madrid: Castalia, 1975), pp. 59–79.

19. *The Golden Age: Drama 1492–1700* (London: Ernest Benn Ltd., 1971), p. 78.

20. *Los Médicis de Florencia* in *BAE* 45:215–36.

21. *The Golden Age: Drama 1492–1700*, p. 78.

22. See note 17.

23. Both *La mayor hazaña de Carlos V* and *Santa Margarita* appear in *Parte treinta y tres de doze comedias famosas de diferentes autores* (Valencia: Claudio Macé, 1642).

24. William A. Kincaid, "Life and Works of Luis de Belmonte Bermúdez (1587?–1650?)," *Revue Hispanique* 74 (1928):1–160; see p. 42.

25. *El diablo predicador* in *BAE* 45:327–46.

26. *El sastre del Campillo,* ed. Frederick A. DeArmas (Chapel Hill, N.C.: Estudios de Hispanófila, 1975).

27. *La renegada de Valladolid* in *BAE* 45:347–66.

Chapter Four

1. For verification of the striking qualities of these works see the introduction to A. D. Kossoff's edition of *El castigo sin venganza* (Madrid: Castalia, 1970): A. Zamora Vicente's edition of *Las bizarrías de Belisa* (Madrid: Espasa-Calpe, 1963); and the introduction to John B. Wooldridge's edition of *El amor enamorado* (Madrid: Porrúa-Turanzas, 1978).

2. These figures are based on the work of Harry W. Hilborn, *A Chronology of the Plays of D. Pedro Calderón de la Barca* (Toronto: University of Toronto Press, 1938). See the summaries he provides on pp. 73–74 and 114.

3. Jack H. Parker, *Juan Pérez de Montalván* (Boston: G. K. Hall, 1975).

4. *Montalbán: un commediografo dell' età di Lope* (Pisa: Università di Pisa, 1970).

5. The best guide to Vélez's theater is still the work of Forrest Spencer and Rudolph Schevill, *The Dramatic Works of Luis Vélez de Guevara* (Berkeley: University of California Press, 1937). Those interested in the *comedia* look expectantly to the forthcoming edition of his complete dramatic works now being prepared by C. George Peale and William Manson.

6. *Francisco de Rojas Zorrilla* (New York: G. K. Hall, 1968), p. 17.

7. Earlier examples of the same tendency might be found in Juan Ruiz de Alarcón's *La verdad sospechosa* ("Truth Suspect") that is, to a large extent, a study of the character of a liar or his *Don Domingo de Don Blas,* in which he deals with an inveterate Epicurean. Both plays belong to the middle years of the decade 1621–1630.

8. Two of the most interesting sources for information about Enríquez Gómez are I. Révah, "Un Pamphlet contre l'Inquisition d'Antonio Enríquez Gómez: La Seconde Parte de la 'Política Angélica' (Rouen, 1647)," *Révue des Etudes Juives (NS)* 4:1 (1962):83–168; and that provided by Constance H. Rose in *Antonio Enríquez Gómez: Fernán Méndez Pinto: Comedia Famosa en Dos*

Partes, Louise G. Cohen, Francis M. Rogers, and C. H. Rose, eds. (Cambridge, Mass.: Harvard University Press, 1974), pp. 47–73.

9. Shergold, p. 297.

10. Ibid., pp. 225–35, 264–97.

11. Ibid., pp. 298–305.

12. These are Rodrigo de Herrera y Ribera, Cristóbal de Monroy y Silva, Antonio Coello y Ochoa, Jerónimo de Cáncer Velasco, Francisco Antonio de Meneses, and Pedro Rosete Niño.

13. The most complete study of Mendoza's life and works is Gareth A. Davies, *A Poet at Court: Antonio Hurtado de Mendoza* (Oxford: Dolphin Book Co., 1971).

14. Davies, p. 225.

15. *Cada loco con su tema* is preserved in an autograph manuscript (Res. 93) in the National Library in Madrid but is most accessible in *BAE* 45:457–76.

16. Gareth Davies, "A Chronology of Antonio de Mendoza's Plays," *Bulletin of Hispanic Studies* 48 (1971):104–106.

17. The exceptionally well-written and sensible book by Davies is marred by his misreading of the denouement of this play. He believes that the foolish Leonor gets what she deserves by being married to Julián. That is not the case. She is married to *Montañés* and Julián is left as the butt of a joke. The error is a serious one since it leads to a complete misinterpretation of the play. Davies also repeatedly refers to Aldonza as Aldonanza. See Davies, pp. 249–56, especially p. 252.

18. *BAE* 45:437–55.

19. *BAE* 45:421–36.

20. Davies, p. 267.

21. *Flor de las mejores doze comedias de los mayores ingenios de España* (Madrid: Diego Díaz de Carrera, 1692), fols. 25–42v.

22. *Más merece quien más ama,* in *Escongidas, parte 46,* pp. 197–213; *Los riesgos que tiene un coche* in *Comedias de Lope de Vega Carpio, Parte veinte y seis* (Zaragoza, 1645); *Galán sin dama* in *Mejor de los mejores libros que ha salido de comedias* (Alcalá: María Fernández, 1651), pp. 170–206; *El premio de la virtud* (*suelta,* n.p., n.d.); *Celos sin saber de quien* (*suelta,* n.p., n.d.).

23. See Davies, pp. 103, 106.

24. Vatican Library, *Barberini Latini,* codex 3481.

25. *The Dramatic Works of Alvaro Cubillo de Aragón,* North Carolina Studies in the Romance Languages and Literatures, 149 (Chapel Hill, N.C.: Department of Romance Languages, 1975).

26. *BAE* 47:79–110.

27. *El justo Lot* and *El mejor rey del mundo* are both known only through individually published copies that date from the eighteenth century.

28. *Los triunfos de San Miguel* was published in Cubillo's *El enano de las musas* ("The Dwarf of the Muses") (Madrid: María de Quiñones, 1654).

29. *Los desagravios de Cristo* is found in *Parte treinta y dos con doze comedias de diferentes autores* (Zaragoza, 1640).

30. *BAE* 47:145–60.

31. *BAE* 47:179–98.

32. *BAE* 47:111–26.

Chapter Five

1. The title is such that it may be read, as well, in reverse order, *The Stars Create Jealousy*. See the edition of this work prepared by John E. Varey, N. D. Shergold, and Jack W. Sage (London: Tamesis, 1970).

2. See Ruth Lee Kennedy, *The Dramatic Art of Moreto* (Northhampton: Smith College Studies in Modern Languages, XIII:1–4, 1931–32) and Frank P. Casa, *The Dramatic Craftsmanship of Moreto* (Cambridge, Mass.: Harvard University Press, 1966).

3. "Because, since the common people pay for them, it is just to speak to them in their own language to give them pleasure." Lope de Vega, *Arte nuevo*, lines 47–48.

4. "If the king speaks, let him imitate in so far as he can, royal gravity; if the old man speaks, let him procure sententious modesty. . . ." Lope de Vega, *Arte nuevo*, lines 268–71. The entire passage (lines 246–83) deals with the problem of decorum in these terms rather than in those of good taste, as we now see it.

5. Wilson and Moir, pp. 139–40.

6. Ed. D. W. Moir (London: Tamesis, 1970).

7. Antonio de Solís y Rivadeneyra, *Amor y obligación*, ed. Eduardo Juliá Martinez (Madrid: Hernando, 1930). See the "Observaciones preliminares," particularly pp. xxxvii–xliii.

8. *BAE* 47:199–218.

9. Published individually with no place, no date.

10. *BAE* 49:195–240.

11. See the study of Diamante's life and works by E. Cotarelo y Mori, *Boletín de la Real Academia Española* 3 (1916):272–97, 454–97.

12. *BAE* 47:361–84.

13. *Comedias nuevas con los mismos saynetes con que se executaron* (Madrid:

Martínez Abad, 1722). Two volumes. Or see also his *Comedias escogidas* (Madrid: Ortega, 1832).

14. See the studies of Salazar y Torres by Thomas A. O'Connor: "Don Agustín de Salazar y Torres," *Bulletin of Bibliography and Magazine Notes* 32 *(1975):*158–62, 167, 180; "Dramatic Use of a *Letra cantada irregular* in *Elegir al enemigo:* A Structural Approach," *Revista de Estudios Hispánicos* 11 (1977):119–32; "Dramatic use of *letras cantadas* in *El amor más desgraciado, Céfalo y Pocris,*" *Bulletin of the Comediantes* 27 (1975):35–40; "An Allusion to Agustín de Salazar y Torres' *Los juegos olímpicos* by Count Harrack," *Romance Notes* 17 (1976):82–83; "The Mythological World of Agustín de Salazar y Torres," *Romance Notes* 18 (1977):221–29; "A Lost Play of Salazar y Torres," *Bulletin of the Comediantes* 25 (1973):40–42.

15. *BAE* 49:265–84.

16. Fernand Braudel, *The Mediterranean and the Mediterranean World in the Age of Philip II* (New York: Harper, 1972), 1:103–67.

17. Gustavo Umpierre, *Songs in the Plays of Lope de Vega* (London: Tamesis, 1975); Jack W. Sage, "Calderón y la música teatral," *Bulletin Hispanique* 58 (1956):275–300; Melvin O. Eubanks, "The Use of Music in the Dramatic Works of Tirso de Molina," Ph.D. dissertation, Florida State University, 1969.

18. "¡Oh, dulces prendas, por mi mal halladas!"

19. *BAE* 49:241–64.

20. Thomas A. O'Connor, "Language, Irony and Death: The Poetry of Salazar y Torres' *El encanto es la hermosura,*" *Romanische Forschungen* 90 (1978):60–69.

21. According to the editor's footnote, this is the point from which Vera Tassis claims to have completed Salazar's work.

22. Gerard Flynn, *Sor Juana Inés de la Cruz* (Boston: G. K. Hall, 1971).

23. *BAE* 49:285–303. Much of what follows here is taken from my own previously published study, "Forma simétrica en las comedias barrocas de Sor Juana Inés," *Cuadernos Americanos* 38:3 (1979):183–93.

24. Sor Juana Inés de la Cruz, *Obras completas,* ed. Francisco Monterde (México: Porrúa, 1969), pp. 714–74.

25. Margaret Sayers Peden, "Sor Juana Inés de la Cruz: The Fourth Labyrinth," *Bulletin of the Comediantes* 27 (1975):41–48.

26. Wilson and Moir, p. 142.

27. Ignacio de Luzán, *La poética o reglas de la poesía,* ed. Luigi de Filippo (Barcelona, 1956), 2:125.

28. *BAE* 49:369–89.

29. *BAE* 49:305–25.

30. *BAE* 49:327–48.

31. *BAE* 49:349–68. For a discussion of Belmonte Bermúdez's work, see

Chapter 3.

32. See the discussion of this point provided in my introduction to Mira de Amescua's *La casa del tahur* (Chapel Hill, N.C.: Estudios de Hispanófila, 1973), especially the section devoted to the play's structure, pp. 24–27.

Selected Bibliography

PRIMARY SOURCES

Dramáticos contemporáneos a Lope de Vega. 2 vols.; *Dramáticos posteriores a Lope de Vega*. 2 vols. Edited by Ramón de Mesonero Romanos (*BAE* 43, 45, 47, 49). Madrid: M. Rivadeneyra, 1857–1859. Since the series *Biblioteca de Autores Españoles* is still in print, these four volumes are the most easily accessible source for ninety *comedias* written by the minor dramatists who are the subject of this study.

Paz y Melia, A. *Catálogo de las piezas de teatro que se conservan en el Departamento de Manuscritos de la Biblioteca Nacional*. Madrid: Patronato de la Biblioteca Nacional, 1934–1935. Prepared under the direction of Paz y Melia, the catalog carefully describes each manuscript. Volume I lists the manuscripts of plays written through the seventeenth century. The first edition of the catalog (1899) does not give the library's location numbers for the manuscripts.

Regueiro, José M., *Spanish Drama of the Golden Age; A Catalogue of the "Comedia" Collection in the University of Pennsylvania Libraries*. New Haven, Conn.: Research Publications, 1971. Because the catalog describes the contents of the microfilmed collection that is also available through the publisher, it is an invaluable resource for locating and obtaining the texts of wanted plays.

Simón Diaz, José. *Bibliografía de la Literatura Hispánica*. Madrid: CSIC, 1950–in publication. See particularly volume IV, in which the early collections of *comedias* are analyzed and a location is cited for copies available. As more volumes are published, the later numbers that deal with authors in alphabetical order (Volume 10 deals with the "G's") will become more and more useful.

SECONDARY SOURCES

1. General Background on the *Comedia*
Barrera y Leirado, Cayetano de la. *Catálogo bibliográfico y biográfico del Teatro*

Antiguo Español, desde sus orígenes hasta mediados del siglo XVIII. Madrid: M. Rivadeneyra, 1860. This is still the best general resource for information about a large number of Golden Age dramatists and their works. It is the starting point for nearly all searches. A facsimile reprint was made: London: Tamesis, 1972.

Díaz Plaja, Guillermo, ed. *Historia General de las Literaturas Hispánicas*. Barcelona: Barna, 1949–in publication. An important collection of monographic essays prepared by leading scholars in a variety of areas and published in volumes arranged chronologically, the work is basic to all study of Spanish literature. Because the sections are individually prepared, they tend to overlap and, at times, contradict each other; therefore caution must be used. The volume of interest to those dealing with the *comedia* is third in the series. The major figures receive overwhelming attention; still, *III:* pp. 285–98 are of interest to those seeking information on the minor dramatists.

Hurtado y Jiménez de la Serna, Juan, and González Palencia, Angel. *Historia de la literatura española*. Madrid: Revista de Archivos, Bibliotecas y Museos, 1925. A basic literary history that, even capsulized as it is, manages to include succinct literary discussion of outstanding works by a wide variety of authors, including most of those studied here.

Sánchez Escribano, Federico, and Porqueras Mayo, Alberto. *Preceptiva dramática española del renacimiento y el barroco. Segunda edición muy ampliada*. Madrid: Gredos, 1972. A valuable anthology of texts dealing with dramatic theory from the fifteenth through the seventeenth centuries, the collection also contains several essays by the editors that deal with the matter of dramatic theory.

Shergold, N. D. *A History of the Spanish Stage*. Oxford: Clarendon Press, 1967. The best general history of the staging practices of the Spanish Golden Age, this work deals only in passing with literary aspects of the drama.

Valbuena Prat, Angel. *Historia del teatro español*. Barcelona: Noguer, 1956. Combining studies of stagecraft with those of dramatic literature, Valbuena Prat's work is a basic reference for all studies of the Spanish theater.

Wilson, Margaret. *Spanish Drama of the Golden Age*. Oxford: Pergamon, 1969. A short review of the major figures and the most important dramatic tendencies designed for those who want a quick, overall view of the Spanish Golden Age theater, the intelligent arrangement and lucid explanations of this little manual make it an invaluable resource for those interested.

2. Bibliography of Publications on the *Comedia*
Published each fall in the *Bulletin of the Comediantes*, this extensive bibliography is arranged alphabetically by author or theme treated. Begun under the leadership of Peter Bell, the bibliography has been prepared since his death by Warren T. McCready (1971–1972), Vern G. Williamsen (1973 to date) and with the collaboration of John J. Reynolds since 1978.

3. The Individual Dramatists
Listed here are materials *not* cited in the footnotes to the various chapters of the text.

Bances y López-Candamo, Francisco Antonio de: Francisco Cuervo Arango. *Don Francisco Antonio de Bances y López-Candamo: Estudio biobibliográfico y crítico* (Madrid: Hernández, 1916) N. Díaz de Escobar. "Poetas dramáticos del siglo XVII: Don Francisco Bances Candamo." *Boletín de la Real Academia de la Historia* 91 (1927):105–14. W. S. Jack. "Bances Candamo and the Calderonian Decadents." *PMLA* 44 (1929):1079–89. Duncan Moir. "Bances Candamo's Garcilaso: An Introduction to *El César africano*." *Bulletin of Hispanic Studies* 49 (1972):7–29.

Belmonte Bermúdez, Luis de: Frederick A. de Armas. "La lealtad en *El sastre del Campillo*." *Hispanófila* 43 (1971):9–16. Ruth Lee Kennedy. *"La renegada de Valladolid."* *Romanic Review* 28 (1932):122–34.

Claramonte y Corroy, Andrés de: B. B. Ashcom. "A *terminus ante quem* for the Birth of Claramonte." *Hispanic Review* 5 (1938):158–59. Juan Barceló Jiménez. "Andrés de Claramonte y Juan de Mérida (Notas a la comedia *El valiente negro en Flandes*)." *Libro-homenaje a Antonio Pérez Gómez* (Cieza: . . . la fonte que mana y corre. . . , 1978), 1:53–63. Alva V. Ebersole. "Simbolismo en *Deste agua no beberé* de Claramonte." *Perspectivas de la Comedia* (Chapel Hill: University of North Carolina Department of Romance Languages, 1978), pp. 119–32.

Cubillo de Aragón, Alvaro: Juan B. Avalle Arce. "Lope y Alvaro Cubillo de Aragón." *Nueva Revista de Filología Hispánica* 7 (1953):429–32. Emilio Cotarelo y Mori. "Dramáticos españoles del siglo XVII: Alvaro Cubillo de Aragón." *Boletín de la Real Academia Española* 5 (1918):3–23, 241–80. Edward Glaser. "Alvaro Cubillo de Aragón's *Los desagravios de Christo*." *Hispanic Review* 24 (1956):306–21. John H. Seekamp. "The Dramatic Craftsmanship of Alvaro Cubillo de Aragón and the Sources for Some of His Plays." Ph.D. (unpublished), Rutgers University, 1974.

Enríquez Gómez, Antonio: Jesús Antonio Cid. "Judaizantes y carreteros para un hombre de letras: Antonio Enríquez Gómez (1600–1663)." In *Homenaje a Julio Caro Baroja* (Madrid: Centro de Investigaciones Sociológicas, 1978), pp. 271–300. N. Díaz de Escobar. "Poetas dramáticos del siglo XVII: Antonio Enríquez Gómez." *Boletín de la Academia Real de la Historia* 88 (1926):838–44. Glen F. Dille. "Antonio Enríquez Gómez's Honor Tragedy *A lo que obliga el honor.*" *Bulletin of the Comediantes* 30 (1978):97–111. ————. "Antonio Enríquez Gómez Alias Fernando de Zárate." *Papers in Language and Literature* 14 (1978):11–21. David M. Gitlitz. "La angustia vital de ser negro. Tema de un drama de Fernando de Zárate." *Segismundo* 11 (1975):65–85. Constance H. Rose. "Antonio Enríquez Gómez and the Literature of Exile." *Romanische Forschungen* 85 (1973):63–77.

Godínez, Felipe: José M. Bella. "Origen y difusión de la leyenda de Pedro Telonario y sus derivaciones en el teatro del Siglo de Oro (Mira de Amescua y Felipe Godínez)." *Revista de Filología Española* 55 (1972): 51–60.

Jiménez de Enciso, Diego: Emilio Cotarelo y Mori. "Don Diego Jiménez de Enciso y su teatro." *Boletín de la Real Academia Española* 1 (1914):209–48, 385–415, 510–50. J. P. W. Crawford. "*El Príncipe don Carlos* of Jiménez de Enciso." *Modern Language Notes* 22 (1907):238–41. Andrée Mansau. "'Meutre dans la tapisserie': version espagnole." *Littératures* (Université de Toulouse–Le Mirail) 23 (1976):41–52. Rudolph Schevill. "The *Comedias* of Diego Jiménez de Enciso." *PMLA* 18 (1903):194–210.

Juana Inés de la Cruz, Sor: L. K. Delano. "The Influence of Lope de Vega upon Sor Juana Inés de la Cruz." *Hispania* 13 (1930):79–94. J. Jiménez Rueda. *Sor Juana Inés de la Cruz en su época* (Mexico: Porrúa, 1951). Claire Pailler. "La question d'amour dan le théâtre profane de Sor Juana Inés de la Cruz." *TILAS* 13–14 (1973–74):60–80. María Esther Pérez. *Lo americano en el teatro de Sor Juana Inés de la Cruz* (New York: Eliseo Torres and Sons, 1975). Rodolfo Usigli. "El teatro de Sor Juana." *El Libro y el Pueblo* 10 (1932):8–11.

Salazar y Torres, Agustín de: Thomas A. O'Connor. "La desmitificación de Celestina en *El encanto es la hermosura* de Salazar y Torres." In *'La Celestina' y su contorno social.* Edited by M. Criado de Val. Barcelona: Hispam, 1977, pp. 399–405.

Salucio del Poyo, Damián: Justo García Soriano. "Damián Salucio del Poyo." *Boletín de la Real Academia Española* 13 (1926):269–82, 474–506. James J. Jewell. "The Plays of Damián Salucio del Poyo." Ph.D. diss. (unpublished), University of New Mexico, 1974.

Sánchez, Miguel: Hugo A. Rennert. "Miguel Sánchez, *El Divino.*" *Modern Language Notes* 8 (1893):131–44. Vern G. Williamsen. "El teatro de Miguel Sánchez, *el divino.*" *Actas del Sexto Congreso Internacional de Hispanistas* (Toronto: Department of Spanish and Portuguese, University of Toronto, 1980), pp. 803–807.

Index

DATE DUE
